TAROT READING EASY GUIDE FOR BEGINNERS

Tarot Mastery, Psychic Tarot Reading, Common Tarot Spreads, Major Arcana, Minor Arcana, Clearing Your Tarot Deck, Tarot Card Meanings, History, Symbolism, and Divination

By Shelly O'Bryan

Copyright 2019 by Shelly O'Bryan - All rights reserved. No part of this book may be reproduced or transmitted in any form or by any means, electronic or mechanical, including photocopying, recording or by any information storage and retrieval system without written permission of the publisher, except for the inclusion of brief quotations in a review.

This content is provided with the sole purpose of providing relevant information on a specific topic for which every reasonable effort has been made to ensure that it is both accurate and reasonable. Nevertheless, by purchasing this content, you consent to the fact that the author, as well as the publisher, are in no way experts on the topics contained herein, regardless of any claims as such that may be made within. As such, any suggestions or recommendations that are made within are done so purely for entertainment value. It is recommended that you always consult a professional prior to undertaking any of the advice or techniques discussed within.

This is a legally binding declaration that is considered both valid and fair by both the Committee of Publishers Association and the American Bar Association and should be considered as legally binding within the United States.

The reproduction, transmission, and duplication of any of the content found herein, including any specific or extended information will be done as an illegal act regardless of the end form the information ultimately takes. This includes copied versions of the work both physical, digital and audio unless express consent of the Publisher is provided beforehand. Any additional rights reserved.

Furthermore, the information that can be found within the pages described forthwith shall be considered both accurate and truthful when it comes to the recounting of facts. As such, any use, correct or incorrect, of the provided information will render the Publisher free of responsibility as to the actions taken outside of their direct purview. Regardless, there are zero scenarios where the original author or the Publisher can be deemed liable in any fashion for any damages or hardships that may result from any of the information discussed herein.

Additionally, the information in the following pages is intended only for informational purposes and should thus be thought of as universal. As befitting its nature, it is presented without assurance regarding its prolonged validity or interim quality. Trademarks that are mentioned are done without written consent and can in no way be considered an endorsement from the trademark holder.

TABLE OF CONTENTS

Introduction 1
Chapter 1 *What Can Tarot Do For You* 3
Chapter 2 *Tarot Through The Ages* 7
Chapter 3 *Where To Begin* 12
Chapter 4 *Learning The Major Arcana* 23
Chapter 5 *Beginning The Minor Arcana* 52
Chapter 6 *The Suit Of Cups* 61
Chapter 7 *The Suit Of Wands* 70
Chapter 8 *The Suit Of Swords* 78
Chapter 9 *The Suit Of Pentacles* 86
Chapter 10 *Starting Simple* 93
Chapter 11 *Complex Layouts* 104
Chapter 12 *Enhancing And Expanding* 111
Conclusion 118
Description 119

INTRODUCTION

Congratulations on purchasing *Tarot Reading Easy Guide for Beginners*, and thank you for doing so. The world of Tarot is full of mystery, from its history and origins to the methodology of cartomancy; even the symbolic imagery used to decorate the cards can be complex and enigmatic. Many people are intrigued by Tarot and eager to learn but quickly find themselves overwhelmed by the sheer amount of information available to beginners. They may be even further confused to find that there are varying opinions on nearly every aspect of Tarot culture--history, best practices, deck preferences, spreads, and card meanings. This is an art form with no right or wrong answers, so novices can often feel as though they are taking a solo pencil dive into the middle of the ocean without a life preserver.

If you've been intimidated, overwhelmed, or confounded by previous attempts to learn Tarot, rest assured--this is the right book for you! Within these pages, you will find every tool you need to get started on reading Tarot, whether you aim to use it for fun and entertainment, serious divination, card collection, or even to jump-start a business centered on metaphysical healing and cartomancy.

Tarot is a useful tool for gaining insight into one's surroundings, as well as for deep introspection. Skeptics of the esoteric and metaphysical energies can still stand to gain a great deal from Tarot, and benefit from readings on philosophical, psychological, and anthropological levels.

There is no right or wrong way to dive into your Tarot practice; this book simply aims to organize the information in an accessible and easily digestible manner. Though the cards often deal with grave subject matter, the process of learning Tarot should be fun, first and foremost. Don't push yourself to study too hard; find someplace comfortable to relax and unwind as you read, and let the information wash over you. Your intuition is the most powerful tool for cartomancy; information from external sources should influence or reflect your intuitive understanding of the cards, rather than overruling it. As you practice, keep yourself loose, open, and relaxed; the goal is to enjoy the experience.

There are plenty of books about Tarot reading on the market, so thank you again for choosing this one! Every effort was made to ensure it is full of as much useful and accurate information as possible. Please enjoy!

CHAPTER 1
What Can Tarot Do For You

What is Tarot?

Tarot cards have existed for hundreds of years, and there are countless editions of the Tarot deck in existence. While the standard playing-card deck contains fifty-two cards of four suits (clubs, diamonds, hearts, and spades), the Tarot deck has seventy-eight cards in total. There are four suits in a Tarot deck, though they differ from those of standard playing decks, usually featuring Cups, Wands, Swords, and Pentacles (though some decks may use Coins or Staves as an alternative). Within each suit, the Tarot deck has four Court Cards--a Page, Knight, Queen, and King--juxtaposed with the three Court Cards in a fifty-two-card deck (the Jack, Queen, and King). Additionally, the Tarot deck features twenty-two additional trump cards (also called "triumph cards") that make up the Major Arcana, whereas the suit and court cards are collectively referred to as the Minor Arcana.

The cards of the Major Arcana are numbered, and feature detailed illustrations of archetypal symbols; though the earliest Tarot decks were designed in a world where organized religion was ubiquitous and inescapable, and many decks feature religious imagery to this day, the symbols used to illustrate the Major Arcana cards are meant to be instantly recognizable in cultures throughout the world, eliciting visceral reactions and drawing meaning from the collective subconscious. As an example, the Wheel of Fortune card includes imagery from Judeo-Christian cultures, as well as ancient Egyptian symbols, and mythical creatures from Pagan and Norse mythologies, with a combination of written English language, Hebrew, and Zodiac symbols at its center.

The numbered suit cards usually feature a lot more variety and detail of illustration than the numbered cards in a fifty-two-card playing deck. In some decks, the added detail is abstract, all floral patterns or geometric shapes. In most modern decks used for cartomancy, though, the numbered suit cards are each given unique illustrations of scenes, full of symbolism and rich narrative meaning.

Tarot as a part of life

Tarot cards are quite popular, and most all of us are familiar with them, even if only to a small degree. We see them featured frequently in entertainment media, used by fortune tellers, witches and magicians as part of a supernatural practice, either to see into the future, form a magical barrier for protection, or to summon spirits and entities from other dimensions. In truth, though, the way Tarot is stereotypically portrayed in popular media is inaccurate, or at the very least, highly exaggerated. We often see protagonists of films visiting a clairvoyant or cliché gypsy character in order to discern the next steps of their journey or uncover an important secret; the cartomancer will usually pull an easily recognizable trump card of the Major Arcana from the deck (the Lovers, Death, and the Devil seem to be the most commonly used cards in popular media) and jump to dire conclusions immediately upon seeing it. Usually, the interpretation of these cards is quite literal: the Lovers signify the beginning of a new romantic affair; Death implies a true loss of life, looming just around the corner; and the Devil is a sign that something wicked is at work in the protagonist's world.

If you're just getting started, dipping your toes into the world of Tarot and metaphysical spirituality, you'd be wise to let go of the expectation of a similar experience; otherwise, you'll be setting yourself up for disappointment. Tarot can indeed be an immensely powerful, life-changing tool, but any experienced reader knows that it's rare to encounter a single card that can accurately predict a romantic development, death, or any other specific future event. Every single card in the deck has multiple potential interpretations--for example, the Death card is much more likely to reference change or figurative rebirth than it is to refer to a literal death, and depending on the context provided by surrounding cards, it can often deliver a message of positivity and optimism for the querent's future. This being the case, it's important for any Tarot enthusiast to remain open-minded and ready to embrace complexity. In the world of divination through Tarot, there is very little black and white; most of the practice resides in a grey area, and no matter how experienced a reader may be, the deck will always have something new to teach them.

Tarot decks don't have much in common with tools like Ouija boards in terms of their connection to the afterlife and deceased spirits, so it's unfortunate that so many stories use Tarot and Ouija interchangeably as a plot device or mechanism to bring ghosts and demonic spirits into the narrative. There is nothing inherently supernatural, spooky, or dark about these cards or the practice of cartomancy. Some cartomancers do prefer to use Tarot as a tool to connect themselves more deeply to the occult, the mystical and mysterious, and the unseen world, but at the same time, there are those who use the cards exclusively for gameplay. Some cartomancers perform divination rites that are designed to ward off negativity of any kind, with no interest in the supernatural or spirit world, using their insight and foresight to provide sitters with mundane life advice (for instance, "Wait till next month to buy that car you've had your eye on," or "schedule some time for yourself this weekend to relax and recharge, because you'll need your energy next week"). Some may use Tarot cards as part of their self-care routine or manifestation rituals; some look to the cards as a sort of living, changing, ever-evolving holy text.

Tarot is for everyone. While it has been historically influenced by philosophical and spiritual trends, Tarot itself isn't connected to any single religion or dogma. Though occult-oriented decks have existed for hundreds of years, the original Tarot decks held no more mystery or darkness than a standard fifty-two card deck of playing cards, and there are plenty of modern decks designed with decidedly light-hearted illustrations. While many turn to Tarot with an interest in seeing into the future, there are those who do not believe the cards harness any type of clairvoyant power; instead, they may use the cards as a means of introspection and self-understanding, much like a psychologist using a Rorschach test to gain insight into a patient's psyche. At the end of the day, Tarot is what you make of it, and the cards can only be as powerful as your belief in them.

How to get the most out of this book

It can often be overwhelming for novices to get started, especially if they feel the need to first memorize the meanings of each card in the Tarot deck; after all, there are 78 unique cards, and every one of them can be impacted or altered by its direction and placement, the cards surrounding it, the context of the spread and the question that prompts it. But rest assured--this book is designed for both novices and experienced practitioners to get the most use out of it. If you are new to the world of Tarot and eager to get started, feel free to skip around in the book, jumping from the third chapter to the tenth and using the chapters in between to look up the possible meanings of each card while you practice. Alternatively, if you already have some familiarity with Tarot divination, you might find it more useful to read straight through from start to finish. Either way, it's a good idea to get yourself started with a Tarot journal, where you can jot down notes, record your card spreads and questions, and even make a note of other aspects of your intuitive practices--numerology, astrology, palmistry, tasseography, crystal scrying, and even dream journaling can all be incorporated into your metaphysical practice and used to deepen your understanding of the cards, enhancing your connection to them.

There is a lot to learn, so you shouldn't expect to become a functional reader overnight. At the same time, much of your talent for cartomancy will come from handling the cards, making your own observations about the illustrations in your deck, and building a personal connection to them, so don't wait to become an expert on the Major and Minor Arcana before you get your hands on a deck. Furthermore, keep in mind that all the spreads listed in this book are simply commonly accepted practices; there are no hard rules in Tarot, and as such, any cartomancer should feel free to experiment with innovative spreads and techniques, even if they are a novice. The sky's the limit, and the only authority you must listen to is your own inner voice.

CHAPTER 2
Tarot Through The Ages

There are several popular versions of Tarot's history, many of which have never been proven to be factual. Some believe the cards originated in ancient Egypt; some believe they were a relic found by the Knights Templar, while others still believe they were originally created in Morocco. Some believe they are of purely European invention, first used in Italy or France. Others may claim that Tarot was invented by Gypsies hailing from India or the Middle East, or a tool used first by Jewish Kabbalists; alternatively, it may have come to us from the Sufis or Cathars. There are some who would even claim the first deck was of divine origin--a gift from a higher power.

Perhaps the origins of the deck are purposefully shrouded in mystery. In this chapter, we'll explore the proven history of Tarot, as well as the unproven myths and legends surrounding its origin. While the evidence commonly accepted by historians and scholars points to a fairly mundane beginning, not at all related to the occult or supernatural, nor divine mystery, the proven history does not necessarily rule out the possibility that the mystical stories are rooted in ancient truths.

Proven History

Historians have yet to find hard proof of the circumstances under which Tarot was first created, but there is a great deal of evidence of its use in Italy as early as the year 1440. The first decks of traditional playing cards came to Europe in the late 1300s from Islamic regions, most likely as a translation of a Turkish card game called "Mamluk." It seems likely that Tarot cards were first created for the purposes of gameplay, serving as trump cards to overrule numbered suit and court cards. They were added to the numbered suit cards to make expanded decks, called "carte da trionfi."

A reference to these "trionfi" cards, or trump cards, was recorded in the court records of Florence in the year 1440. The word "Tarot" doesn't appear in any historical written records until the year 1530, by which point the cards had gained popularity in parlor rooms and gambler's halls throughout Italy, France, and Portugal. Interestingly, the word "Tarot" does not derive from the word "trionfi," but rather from the Italian word "tarocchi," which is the plural of "tarocco." As a noun, tarocco means "blood orange," and as an adjective, it means "forged" or "fraudulent." The term "taroch" was also commonly used as slang in the fifteenth and sixteenth centuries, to describe silliness, brouhaha, or foolish behavior.

The cards seemed to serve a variety of purposes in Europe over the next century. They were used in a game called "triumph," a name which eventually changed to "tarocchi" or "tarocchini." This game is still played in certain regions of Italy to this day. These games are similar to bridge or whist. There was also a game called "tarocchi appropriati" played using only the trump cards (now known as the Major Arcana) in which a lineup of cards would be dealt at random for a sitter; the dealer would then use thematic interpretations of the cards' illustrations to compose poetic verses about other players on the spot. This was a playful, joking game, in which the verses would often describe the fates or futures of the chosen subject, much like the modern children's game M.A.S.H. These future predictions were not meant to be taken as serious divination in this context. The game was about fun and humor, perhaps flirtation; not mysticism or clairvoyance.

As these games gained popularity throughout the European continent, many wealthy courtiers and nobles began to commission their own artistically unique decks, and thus regional variations in design and gameplay became quite common. While many modern decks have incorporated mystical, occult, ancient Egyptian, feminist, and new age symbolism, Tarot decks from this time period generally reflected the realities of everyday life in their illustrations. There was a great deal of explicitly Christian imagery, primarily reflective of Roman Catholic traditions and values. The suit of Pentacles was then a suit of Coins; Wands were usually Polo Sticks, Batons, or Staves.

It wasn't until the late 18th century that Tarot cards were designed, published, and used for the specific purpose of cartomancy, mystical and arcane study, and metaphysical workings. In the previous decades, occult communities in Europe began using the

Tarot de Marseilles deck, which was previously used for gameplay, for divination. The idea was popularized by Antoine Court de Gebelin and Jean-Baptiste Alliette (also known as Etteila) in Paris in the early 1780's; the team then went on to issue the first esoteric Tarot deck and accompanying manual in 1789, claiming its symbolism drew heavily from the magical, hermetic knowledge recorded in the ancient Egyptian Book of Thoth. This was enthusiastically received by the growing occult community.

All of this is recorded in history, but the picture it paints is incomplete. It's entirely possible that Tarot has no mystical or supernatural origins, and was simply a card game that grew into something much more complex over time. At the same time, it's also quite possible that this history tells us only a small fraction of the complete story; perhaps Tarot's true origins and colloquial use were never recorded on paper, as the cards were used by the poor, travelers, religious apostates, and people in hiding from the law or the church.

Myths, Legends, and Lore

Many believe that the written history of Tarot eschews an important aspect of the deck's origins: who was the first to create the Tarot, or bring it to Europe, before the written records of the Visconti-Sforza deck appeared? It seems impossible that the concept of Tarot could have appeared in the court of the Duke of Milan in the 15th century all of a sudden, as though spontaneously generated there; most likely, Tarot decks were in circulation amongst common people for some time before this proof was stamped into the historical record. We are still left to wonder how exactly the deck came to be embraced by the Italian nobility in the first place. The imagery seems too complex and rich with meaning to have been originally designed for a frivolous parlor game.

Some believe that it was the Gypsies, or Rom people, who first brought the Tarot deck to Europe on their travels through the Middle East. This is evidenced by the fact that to this day, some Rom people use the Tarot deck as a Holy Text, as well as a tool for divination. It would make sense that no written records of such an event exist, as the Rom people were largely shunned in Europe, forced to travel constantly, pack light, and develop a culture of secrecy for the sake of protection.

There are also those who would claim it was the Knights Templar who brought the first Tarot decks back to Europe with them as they returned from the Crusades. Some believe it was due to the magic of the Tarot that the Knights Templar were able to achieve so much success and wealth upon their return, gaining the people's favor rather suddenly. Of course, there is no written evidence to support this theory, as there is little surviving evidence to prove any of the Templar legends true or false.

There are some schools of thought which claim the origins of the Tarot deck might be traced back to the early initiation rites of Christian Gnostic sects, also known as Cathars; or, perhaps the deck was created by Jewish or Christian Kabbalists. Some theories posit that the twenty-two cards of the Major Arcana are correlated to the twenty-two letters of the Hebrew alphabet; this theory is challenged, though, by historical evidence that many early Tarot decks only features twenty-one triumph cards, leaving out the Fool.

One popular story explains that the first Tarot deck was created by a group of mystics in Fez, Morocco, in the middle ages, as a means of preserving the esoteric, cabalistic, and arcane texts that were lost in the destruction of the Great Library of Alexandria (a historical event which is also shrouded in a fair amount of mystery, in and of itself). These mystics allegedly recorded the information in code, in order to prevent detection by the Roman Catholic church, which was extraordinarily powerful at the time and eager to stamp out all pagan and alternative belief systems. Since these mystics would have needed to keep their actions hidden and secret, it's unlikely that any historical proof of this story will ever surface, whether it is true or false.

Modern Tarot Culture

Whatever the true history of Tarot may be, one thing is for certain: its popularity is growing steadily, and decks are constantly being updated, modernized, and altered to reflect present-day realities and value systems. These days, many people collect Tarot decks and practice divination without harboring any belief in the supernatural or metaphysical; meanwhile, there are still those who believe strongly in the energetic power of the cards and use them for geomancy spreads and manifestation rituals in addition to cartomancy.

Modern decks often feature feminist slants, racial diversity, references to technology and internet culture, and tend to include more secular imagery in illustrations. There are more varieties of deck styles available now than ever; some are intricate with detailed, hand-drawn illustrations, while others are simplified with minimalist images, sometimes printed in a cartoon or kawaii style.

Modern decks are often designed with the understanding that every person is unique, and the imagery in the popular Rider-Waite deck may not resonate with them, or the situations they encounter in present-day culture. Whatever your perspective, there is most certainly a deck out there that will align with your beliefs, values, and aesthetic preferences.

CHAPTER 3
Where To Begin

We've discussed the past--now it's time to look to the future and get started!

But where should you get started? In this chapter, we'll walk through the basics of acquiring, storing, cleaning and caring for your deck. We'll also look at some tips for awakening your intuition before you try your hand at divination.

If your interest in Tarot is primarily rooted in an appreciation for its history and the ways in which it reflects aspects of human psychology, then there's no need to adhere to the following guidelines. However, if you intend to use the cards for insight, foresight or cartomancy of any kind, it would be wise to keep the following in mind going forward.

Finding your first deck

Traditionally speaking, a first deck should be given to you, not purchased by your own hand. There is no reason why you couldn't ask someone to do this for you if you're anxious to get started; in fact, you might agree to trade decks with another novice, so that you both can say your first Tarot decks were gifts. Once your first deck has been received, you're welcome to expand your collection through personal purchase, but be mindful of the fact that the first cards received may be imbued with the most powerful clairvoyant energies, or maybe the only ones to resonate with your personal energetic frequency. It is also a best practice to give a new deck to another novice after you receive your own, to pay it forward and keep the tradition alive.

Here is a list of some popular Tarot decks you may want to look into as a novice, as well as some more abstract and eccentric decks to look into when it's time to expand your collection.

Decks for novices

Rider-Waite

This is one of the most popular decks in publication today, and it's the deck whose illustrations we'll reference most frequently in this book. For that and many other reasons, it makes an excellent first deck for beginners. Originally published in 1909, the deck was named for publisher William Rider, and A.E. Waite, a prominent public figure in the mystic community at the time. The deck was masterfully illustrated by Pamela Colman Smith, using a combination of traditional Christian imagery, Jewish and Kabbalist symbolism, ancient Egyptian references, and modern feminist slant (or, at least what would have passed for "modern feminism" during this era). The deck set itself apart by including an explanatory booklet with a guide to divination, and by illustrating the numbered suit cards with unique narrative details to aid in memorization.

There are several versions of this deck in publication, some with more radiant or muted color schemes, some in larger or smaller card sizes, and many special editions. There's even a set that glows in the dark!

Thoth Tarot, or Book of Thoth

This is a great deck for beginners who want a bit more esoteric energy in their Tarot practice. Produced by English occultist and magician Aleister Crowley, and painted by Lady Freida Harris under his instruction, this beautiful deck was published alongside a book of the same name, including detailed instructions for divination. This can be a great deck for novices, so long as they know how to translate the updated names of some Major Arcana cards. In the Thoth deck, the Magician is renamed the Magus; the High Priestess is simply the Priestess; Strength is retitled as Lust; the Wheel of Fortune is just Fortune; Justice is renamed Adjustment; Judgment is recast as the Aeon; and finally, the World becomes the Universe.

The Gilded Tarot

Inspired by the classic Rider-Waite imagery with renaissance era characters, but set in the cosmos with a psychedelic, new age twist. It's particularly useful for beginners because the suit cards are color-coded; this helps to get into the practice of associating the corresponding elements to each of the suit cards as you read spreads.

Sun and Moon Tarot

Painted in soft pastels and a folk-art style, this deck is fantastic for those who are new to Tarot, specifically because the numbered suit cards are labeled with clue words--an excellent tool for memorization. It's lovely to look at and features a more racially diverse cast of characters, and some that shake up gender norms of traditional tarot decks.

The Golden Tarot

Designed from collaged medieval and renaissance era artworks, this historic style deck is great for beginners because the images hold so many detailed clues to the cards' meanings. It's a perfect deck for art history lovers, beautifully designed and full of biblical symbolism; for example, the Empress card uses a painting of the Virgin Mary. This deck used a suit of Coins in place of Pentacles.

New Mythic Tarot

Originally published in 1986, this deck draws heavily on the illustrations of the Rider-Waite deck, but has some minor illustrative departures. The deck is re-imagined to feature a cast of characters from ancient Greek myths, adding an extra layer of narrative content to the card meanings. For example, the Star card is drawn to represent a snapshot moment from the myth of Pandora's box, while the Hanged Man is drawn as Prometheus, ready to receive Zeus' punishment.

Morgan Greer Tarot

Loosely based on the Rider-Waite deck, these cards are borderless, full of bright, lush colors, and most characters are drawn in closeup, with features and details well-defined. This is a great deck for those who are new to the world of Tarot, as the artwork is very approachable but still intricate, beautiful, and complex. Designed and published in the 1970s, the Morgan-Greer illustrations hint at the trends of flower power and psychedelia. This is one of very few decks to use a medieval or fantasy era setting while also including racial diversity in the illustrations.

Robin Wood Tarot

This deck is inspired by Rider-Waite but leans heavily upon pagan symbolism rather than Christian religious imagery, so it is a go-to for modern-day pagans, wiccans, and secularists. The illustrations have an ethereal, art-nouveau era style, with a dark fairy tale mood, and bright colors that make the card imagery extremely easy for novices to read.

Decks for experienced readers, collectors, and Tarot lovers

Tarot de Marseilles

This traditional French medieval style deck is a must-have for any collector who loves history. It is one of the oldest deck designs still in popular circulation; its earliest version may have been produced as early as the year 1500; there is a copy of this deck still in existence that was made in 1650. In the Tarot de Marseilles, illustrations of the Major Arcana cards are somehow cartoonishly simplistic and hauntingly beautiful at the same time. The only reason this deck is not ideal for beginners is the design of the numbered suit cards; while they are beautiful and intricate, they often feature geometric designs rather than illustrations and can be difficult for novices to interpret.

Motherpeace Tarot

This is one of the most popular and distinctive modern decks around. It was designed in the 1970s to update the classic Tarot imagery to something better suited to new-wave feminist ideals, particularly inspired by the Goddess movement. The cards are round rather than rectangular; their shape symbolizes the moon and feminine energy. This is a wonderful deck for those who crave a diverse, intersectional, feminist update to Tarot imagery and symbolism. The deck even has its own unique spread of eleven cards laid out in a circular shape.

The Hermetic Tarot

Another great deck for history lovers, and those with a special interest in the esoteric side of Tarot. This deck features a great deal of symbolism from the Secret or Hermetic Order of the Golden Dawn, an occultist group that was popular in Europe at the turn of the twentieth century and still survives to this day (though it boasts lesser numbers currently). While the current Golden Dawn movement may have some unfortunate connections to fascist and racist ideologies, the Hermetic order was primarily concerned with the preservation of ancient alchemical, cabalistic, and arcane knowledge; current leaders of the Hermetic Order claim no connection or alignment whatsoever with the modern Golden Dawn movement. This deck is a wonderful tool to further your study of individual card meanings, as the images feature clues to elemental, astrological, kabbalistic, numerical, and geomantic connections for many cards. The entire deck is drawn in only black and white, with highly detailed illustrations; you'll want to stare at these spreads for hours.

Aquarian Tarot

This deck is breathtakingly beautiful, featuring art deco and art nouveau inspired illustrations and a modern color scheme. The symbolism is a bit more complex than a standard deck, and this isn't ideal for a novice cartomancer, but for a reader who has some experience with a traditional deck, it will be easy to transition into this style.

Shadowscapes Tarot

This is a gorgeous deck, with finely detailed, ethereal illustrations. In fact, the beautiful imagery is the only reason this deck might not work for beginners--it can be a distraction, and furthermore, some of it is quite abstract. This is a great deck for anyone who loves fantasy, Norse mythology, and faeries.

The Wild Unknown Tarot

This beautiful deck is gaining a large modern following. It may not be best for novices, as many of the illustrations are minimalist, featuring nature and animals rather than human characters, but the artist's interpretations of card meanings are profound and inspiring.

Starchild Tarot

A perfect deck for the modern-minded wiccan, this deck uses a gorgeous pastel, new-age color scheme, and photo-collage art to create some truly breathtaking imagery. This deck draws heavily on cosmic spirituality, sacred geometry, metaphysical healing philosophies and ancient mystery schools for symbolism.

Fountain Tarot

Another wonderful modern deck, the Fountain Tarot features original oil paintings by Jonathan Saiz that beautifully capture the concepts of Tarot, updating them for the internet age while retaining a sense of mystery and appreciation for its historical legacy. It's a must-have for modern metaphysical practitioners, energy healers, and contemporary art lovers, too.

Visconti-Sforza Deck

This deck is about as old as the Tarot de Marseilles design, and another wonderful deck for history lovers, with illustrations drawn in more of a medieval style, barely hinting at the dawning of the Renaissance. The original Visconti deck is missing four cards--the Tower, the Devil, the Three of Swords and the Knight of Coins--so for modern prints, these four cards have been recreated in a similar style to the rest of the deck. Many of the original cards survive to this day, in museums and private collections; they were often created using precious materials, such as gold leaf for the card's borders, and show us not only that Tarot was valued by the wealthy and powerful, but also provide us a glimpse into the daily life and value structure of the Italian nobility of the 15th century through its detailed imagery.

Caring for your cards

However, you acquire your deck (or decks), you'll want to store them in a silk cloth or bag, in a cool, dry place. Ideally, you'll want to store them out of direct sunlight, but also avoid storing them in perpetual darkness (basements, dark corners, etc.). If you believe in metaphysical power, then be sure to protect your cards from negative energies, either by storing with a crystal that can combat negativity, keeping the deck within a protection grid or by regularly cleansing the cards.

In order to bond the cards of the deck to your personal spirit, see to it that nobody touches the cards except yourself--even those people whose questions prompt your readings. For this reason, it might be wise to purchase another deck for practice after receiving your first as a gift; that way, you can work with another novice to familiarize yourself with card readings.

Some cartomancers believe that Tarot decks, even when wrapped in silk and out of use, possess the metaphysical energy needed to easily weaken or even open portals between realms; for this reason, some warn that Tarot cards should not be used or even touched during pregnancy, or while a woman is menstruating, and that decks should also be avoided on All Hallow's Eve, on nights with no moon, and any evening after ten o'clock at night, if the reader wishes to avoid communion with any negative energies or malicious spirits.

How to cleanse your cards

Especially after practice or heavy use, you'll want to make sure that you cleanse your decks to remove any negative energy and prevent muddled clarity in the messages you receive from the cards. If you aren't using your Tarot decks frequently, you'll still want to put them through a routine cleanse about once a month; get into the habit of cleansing every new moon, or every full moon if you prefer to use moonlight for cleansing.

To cleanse with moonlight, spread your cards out beneath the light of a full moon and give them time to soak up those moonbeams-- at least an hour per card--before wrapping them in silk again. Another popular cleansing method is smudging, which is a ritual cleansing with smoke. This can be done by burning smudge sticks made of bundled sage leaves, rosemary, or any other dried herb with a scent that you particularly enjoy. Run the cards over the smoke, being sure to separate them so that the smoke can reach every single card, on all surfaces.

Alternatively, some cartomancers prefer to slip their decks into plastic bags or airtight containers before burying the sealed deck in salt (ideally, sea salt or rock salt, but table salt will also work in a pinch), making sure the deck is entirely submerged, and remains buried for several days before being used again. This method takes longer, as the salt will slowly draw negative and stagnant energies from the deck as it would draw moisture from a piece of preserved meat. Be sure to keep the cards protected in an airtight container, as salt and moisture may damage the cards over time.

Awakening your intuition

One of the first steps towards enhancing your intuitive powers is to learn how to recognize them. Many of us make the mistake of thinking that intuition happens in the head or mind, as part of a thought process; that is intellect, not intuition. Intuition happens within the body and subconscious. It often displays itself as strong emotions or physical sensations. An inexplicable sense of optimism, a melancholy mood, or a sudden sharp pain in the gut-- these experiences can all be interpreted as intuitive messages. Meditation and mindfulness practices are excellent tools to heighten your awareness of intuitive experiences and can help to transform you into an astute and insightful card reader, as well as helping you to become the best possible version of yourself in other walks of life.

Lots of people are imbued with many more intuitive gifts than they give themselves credit for, especially since modern life and technologies often encourage us to disconnect from and deny our gut instincts, suppressing physical manifestations of emotion. This being the case, it is usually a good idea for a novice cartomancer to spend some time reflecting upon the imagery in their first deck before they begin a formal study of Tarot. Go through each card in the deck; examine the illustrations; maybe even grip each card with both hands, creating an energetic channel, close your eyes, and breathe. How does the card make you feel? What messages can you divine from it without external guidance? Different decks have different energetic vibes, so while this book will speak to the most commonly accepted interpretations of popular decks, you may find that your cards depict the mysteries of life in a different light, or capture them from a different angle. The colors and shapes used in card illustrations will impact you on a visceral level, and these initial impressions will resonate even more strongly with a reader who gets to know their deck without any preconceived notions or expectations.

Many card practitioners find that they benefit from ritual practices to deepen their connection to their favorite deck, leading to more accurate and insightful readings. You might incorporate your deck into a daily, weekly, or monthly meditation practice, holding the entire deck or just a single selected card as you meditate on its imagery and divine meaning. You might also adopt the practice of sleeping with your deck underneath your pillow (wrapped in silk for protection, of course!) to connect your dreaming, subconscious mind to the cards.

Dream journaling can be extraordinarily helpful in enhancing your awareness of your intuitive mind; it can also aid the novice cartomancer to get into the practice of interpreting imagery and symbolism in abstract sequence. Spending time in nature, relaxing, and regular sleep cycles are immensely important for divination; without a healthy, well-rested mind, even the most experienced card-reader is liable to misunderstand the messages of the divine and their own subconscious.

Sense isolation can be a useful practice for recognizing and honing your sixth sense. Sensory deprivation chambers can provide this experience for a cost, but you needn't shell out any cash to experiment with this practice. Try using makeshift blindfolds, earplugs or nose plugs, or keeping your hands bundled in oven mitts to learn how acute your senses can grow when one or more of the others are diminished. This can help you to recognize where your sensational feelings are coming from, and root out those that have no rational or obvious explanation.

For those who struggle to quiet the mind during meditation, repetitive actions or tasks may be able to provide a similar transcendent experience. This could be running, practicing the performance of one particular song on the guitar or piano and striving for perfection, chopping vegetables to prep meals for the week, doodling, juggling, dancing, or creating origami sculptures. These repetitive motions can lead you into a sort of self-induced hypnosis.

Tension is like a mental fog to a clairvoyant. Find a way to release some before your next reading session. You might choose to do this by seeking an adrenaline rush, taking a yoga class, through laughter or through sexual release. Go to an amusement park, watch a scary movie, or drop in on a dance or improv class. If you prefer to release through relaxation rather than thrill-seeking, you might choose to get a massage or treat yourself to a metaphysical healing session, go for a stroll without a set destination, or take a nice long bath. Finally, if your primary source of emotional anxiety is rooted in a relationship, make it a priority to clear the air. Perhaps you have unexpressed feelings for someone that are plaguing your thoughts, in which case it would be best to make your desires known before a reading; or, you might be feeling frustrations in an existing relationship that need to be addressed in order to clear your head. Whatever the issue, be mindful of the fact that your personal emotions will distract you, preoccupy your thoughts, and ultimately serve to distort or corrupt the messages you receive from the cards, as you will be likely to project your subconscious thoughts onto the cards rather than being able to judge them from the standpoint of objectivity.

Even if there is no major issue or problem on your mind, it will be difficult to harness your intuitive powers if your head is clouded with too much stress or anxiety from daily life. After a release of pent-up energy, you'll find you are more naturally insightful. A stressed or anxious person is often disproportionately focused on the things they fear or desire, which often leaves them unable to see the forest for the trees; but if you are able to effectively clear your energy field on a regular basis, you'll find more clarity of vision, both literal and figurative. You'll find you are attuned to small details while being able to see the big picture simultaneously. Tension causes us to collapse in on ourselves, or occasionally lash out; this is why people suffering from chronic stress or anxiety often have back and neck problems, as well as sour or pinched facial expressions and the body language of a powder keg (arms crossed, shoulders raised to the ears, knees locked, muscles tight). When you find healthy ways to relieve your stress, you'll be able to open yourself up--physically, mentally, emotionally, and metaphysically--and become far more receptive to the divine messages of the universe.

CHAPTER 4
Learning The Major Arcana

The Fool's Journey

When the twenty-two cards of the Major Arcana are arranged upright and in order, the images tell a story that is sometimes referred to as "the Fool's journey." The Fool himself does not make further appearances in other trump cards, and some cards feature female characters exclusively; each card represents a character he encounters or an experience that changes him. The Major Arcana cards are character archetypes, phases of life, or rites of passage that every person must endure and learn from in order to reach a state of metaphysical balance and personal contentment.

Some people find it helpful to create a narrative of the Fool's journey in order to better memorize the meanings of the cards within the Major Arcana, imagining themselves in the Fool's place, meeting each of the characters in order as they give advice and steer the Fool towards divine enlightenment. Following this narrative, you may note that the Fool tends to encounter cards in pairs of dichotomy and contrast, seesawing back and forth between extremes; for example, the Magician and High Priestess represent two opposite takes on creativity and divine power, the first being active while the latter is passive. Next, the Fool meets the Empress and Emperor, juxtaposing the ultimate mother figure with the ultimate father figure, fluidity with rigidity, and pleasure with discipline. This continues in groupings of two to three cards all the way through to the twenty-second card. The chaotic and fearful energy of the Tower is balanced by the hope and reassurance of the Star; the mystery and illusion of the Moon is juxtaposed with the clarity and optimism of the Sun; the Judgement card appears to extract the good from the bad, while the World card comes right behind it to remind the Fool that everything in the universe is connected, and whether good or bad, we are all one with the divine.

Major Arcana cards

As you may remember from the earlier chapter on Tarot's history and origins, the evidence suggests that the Major Arcana cards were created long before the rest of the cards in the deck. Though they have changed over time, their titles and illustrated themes have remained remarkably stable over the past six hundred years. This means that the level of detail in these illustrations, as well as the complexity of their potential interpretations, is far more in-depth than those of the Minor Arcana. You may choose to skip ahead to chapter 10 and begin handling the cards and practicing spreads based on visceral reactions to cards; however, if you do choose to study card meanings before applying yourself to a reading, the Major Arcana is the best place to start.

Keep in mind that different decks will feature varied illustrations and symbolism; if your primary deck features imagery that varies greatly from the descriptions below, take note of the differences, perhaps even jotting your observations down in your Tarot journal. The descriptions in this chapter will be primarily based upon the illustrations featured in the standard Rider-Waite deck, which is one of the most popular modern decks designed for the purpose of divination; this deck's symbolism is influenced by the Tarot's mythical Egyptian roots, whereas earlier decks will feature more prominent Christian symbolism, and modern decks will often draw heavily upon the occult, urban fantasy, or abstract imagery.

The Fool

While the term "fool" has plenty of derogatory implications, such as recklessness or stupidity, there is nothing implicitly negative or piteous in this card's character. In Tarot, the Fool represents the energy of a child: curious, optimistic, playful, eager, and open-minded, with unlimited potential and a lack of preconception or cynicism. Even though some earlier decks depict the Fool as a vagabond in tattered rags, the spirit of this card is carefree, not weighed down by responsibility or the expectations of society, and optimistic. When upright, this card may point towards a fresh start, risky venture, or wild leap of faith in the future. In matters of romance, it can point towards a querent falling blindly in love, or viewing the object of one's affection through rose-colored glasses. In matters of work or finance, it may encourage the querent to take a new career opportunity or dive into a new industry with optimism and enthusiasm.

Reversed - Still indicating a new beginning or fresh start, when the Fool is reversed, it can represent a reluctance to embrace change or tendency towards cynicism and apprehension. A reversed Fool can also predict that change is coming, despite the querants best efforts to maintain the status quo. In matters of love and finance, the reversed Fool card should be taken as a warning to proceed with caution, mind the small details, and read the fine print. Whatever the query, a reversed Fool card can be interpreted as a reminder to pay careful attention to where your feet are taking you, regardless of what's in your head or heart.

Symbolism - In the Rider-Waite deck, the Fool looks like a young daydreamer, wandering dangerously close to the edge of a cliff with his head in the clouds. He is well-dressed, carrying a white rose and a satchel of belongings, followed by a small dog, with his head upturned towards the sunshine and a cascade of mountains in the background.

In earlier Italian or French decks, though, the Fool might be called "Le Mat" or "Il Matto" which translates to "madman" or "beggar," and the illustration will depict quite a different character. He might be drawn as a vagrant, dressed in ragged clothing with a gaunt face, with no flowers in hand or sunshine in the background. In other decks, he may be drawn in a classic court jester's costume, and the dog who serves as a companion in the Rider-Waite illustrations instead bites at his legs or tears at his clothing.

It's important to take note of how your deck depicts the Fool. If he is drawn in an admirable light, it would be wise to focus on the positive implications of an upright card; however, if he is drawn as someone to be mocked, ridiculed, or pitied, then advise your querent to err on the side of caution.

The Magician

Also sometimes labeled as "The Magus" or "The Juggler," the Magician represents the querent's resourcefulness, capability, and personal empowerment. Each of us is endowed with personal skills, talents, and powers; when this card appears face-up in any spread, it serves to remind the querent of these abilities and how they may be useful in addressing current circumstances, combating challenges and surmounting obstacles. It prods us to tap into our fullest potential, looking within rather than focusing on external factors.

The Magician represents power, but not an unlimited amount. It can be tempting to think of him as an all-powerful wizard, but historically, the Magician was a low-ranking card--only one step above the Fool, and called "Le Bateleur" in older French decks, which is a sleight of hand artist, or stage performer. Within a spread, it urges the querent to make use of that which is already at their disposal, and honor their gifts, whatever they may be.

Reversed - When this card is upright, it denotes personal power used to achieve positive ends. Reversed, it can indicate just the opposite: power used for negativity, deceit, and manipulation. This may be a warning to steer clear of a well-laid trap or a charming fraud in your midst. It may also reference a skill or talent that is going to waste, unused or lacking spotlight and amplification. Finally, it can represent a skill or ability that is lacking which will prevent the querent from accomplishing stated goals; for example, a person diving into a new small business venture may have every tool needed for success except one, such as accounting or marketing skills, and the reversed Magician card would serve to remind them that success will remain out of reach until this shortcoming is addressed. Creatively, it could mean a block or lack of inspiration; romantically, professionally, or spiritually, it could mean stagnant or stifled energy.

Symbolism - In the Rider-Waite deck, the Magician appears to be a man, though the card features a female mage in many modern decks. He (or she) stands over a table, upon which rests a cup, a sword, a wand, and a pentagram or coin, each item representing one of the four suits that make up the Tarot deck; this shows us that he has all the tools he needs for creation and transformation at his disposal. He has a scroll in one hand, reaching up towards the universe, while the other hand reaches down towards the earth, symbolizing the magus as conduit from divine energy to the mortal realm; above his head is an infinity symbol (in some representations, his hat makes the shape of a sideways figure eight) and around his waist is a belt made of a snake eating its own tail; both symbolize the potential for limitless power, and the cost of it.

The High Priestess

This card may also be called the Papess or Popess, as the term "High Priestess" would be anachronistic in historically accurate decks designed before the late 1700s. It represents intuition, mystery, and the divine feminine. In an upright position, this card signifies the need to trust in one's gut instincts, keep faith in spiritual wisdom, or to trust in the mystical knowledge of a feminine sage or diviner. It encourages stillness, passivity, and introspection, urging the querent towards a level of inner balance that will allow them to hear their own intuitive voice. Her message is: look within you, not without.

The High Priestess also indicates an enigma: things disguised or hidden, mysteries that have yet to unfold, people, objects, or institutions that are not what they appear to be. This is hinted at in the card's illustration; the High Priestess sits before a temple, but the building itself is hidden behind a patterned veil. When you find this card upright in any spread, it is advisable to trust in your own gut and stay wary of anything that seems particularly tempting, seductive, or too good to be true.

Reversed - When the High Priestess is reversed, it may signify cognitive dissonance, secretiveness, self-doubt, or other intuitive challenges that could be preventing the querent from trusting in their own judgment. It can also represent a duplicitous female or dishonest feminine energy in the querent's life, distorting their perception of reality. In the context of health issues, a reversed High Priestess may indicate a hormonal imbalance or underlying health issue that impacts the querent's mood, capacity for impulse control, and judgment.

No matter the context or question, a reversed High Priestess is most often an urgent call for self-care. The querent needs to focus on reconnecting to the self and getting in touch with their inner voice and core desires.

Symbolism - In the Rider-Waite deck, the High Priestess is depicted as Shekhinah, the female embodiment of the divine. She sits between two pillars of Solomon's Temple, labeled with the letters J and B, standing for Jachin and Boaz, one light and one dark, symbolizing a balance of dualities, masculine and feminine, good and evil; a crescent moon rests at her feet, and upon her head is a horned crown, similar to that of Egyptian Goddess Hathor. She wears blue robes, a white solar cross over her chest, and holds a scroll with the word "Torah" written upon it, which means "divine law." Behind her is a veil that disguises the Temple, covered in pomegranates (a symbol of fertility) and green leaves; further behind that, you'll glimpse a body of water.

In earlier decks, the High Priestess or Papess might be depicted in a more traditionally religious light, wearing a Papal tiara with modest vestments and a Holy Bible in hand. In many modern decks, the High Priestess is renamed as "the Seer" and may be depicted as an androgynous or gender fluid being. No matter the era, this card always references inner knowledge and some form of divine wisdom.

The Empress

The Empress is overflowing with feminine creative energy. She is maternal, sensual, creative, lustrous, abundant, and powerful. Unlike the High Priestess, she is firmly rooted in the pursuit of earthly pleasures. When upright, this card has a strong connection to motherhood, which can be interpreted to signify a literal pregnancy or childbirth, or a figurative birthing of a creative or professional project.

Reversed - While upright, the Empress wields the ultimate power to reproduce life; when reversed, though, she symbolizes a lack of productivity. This could mean a creative block, professional stagnation, or literal inability to reproduce (or other fertility problems). After a recent birth, it could indicate the onset of postpartum depression or other difficulties in forming a motherly bond with a newborn.

Symbolism - This card is rich with symbolic imagery and color. The Empress sits upon a throne in nature, surrounded by trees, a waterfall, and a field of golden wheat. She wears a crown of twelve stars, one for each of the zodiac signs, and holds a scepter in her raised right hand, reminding us of her power. Her throne is full of pillows--she is clearly quite comfortable. By her feet rests a heart-shaped shield with the sign of Venus engraved upon it: a symbol of love and protection. Her long, flowing robes feature a print that is reminiscent of the veiled background in the High Priestess card, full of open pomegranates spilling seeds, a symbol to represent fertility.

The Emperor

The Emperor is a symbol of power, leadership, and stability. When upright, this card signifies order, organization, authority, structure and rigid control. While this may not sound like a fun card to encounter, it can be a welcome sight for any querent who is craving security and strength. The Emperor is the ultimate father figure, representing paternal influence in all its forms. He rules with a strict and vigilant eye, and though his laws may be austere, the feelings of safety and satiety that he provides serve to make it all worth it.

When encountering this card upright, you may interpret it as an encouragement to embrace a strict routine in order to pursue goals; for example, if the querent is considering a new dietary regimen to combat health problems, this card may indicate that strict adherence to rules will be necessary to achieve the desired results. Discipline, self-control, and maintenance of strong boundaries will pave the way to success and contentment.

While this card has strong masculine energies and implications, it may still apply to the querent if they do not identify as a male.

Reversed - The flipped Emperor is not able to use his power effectively. This reversed card can point towards a lack of authority, immaturity, or loss of self-control; alternatively, it might point in the opposite direction, towards a hunger for power that is clouding judgment, an obsessive need for control, inappropriate manipulation, and overly rigid rules or boundaries.

Symbolism - In contrast with the relaxed, luxurious, cushioned, reclining throne on the Empress card, the Emperor sits upon a straight, symmetric, uncomfortable looking throne made of gray rock and adorned with ram skulls, a symbol of leadership and connection to Aries. In the background, you'll see a mountain range, symbolizing the strenuous work he's done to reach this point; the mountains also represent unyielding strength and stability. The Emperor wears a suit of armor beneath his red robes, always protected and impassable. He holds an ankh scepter in his right hand, symbolizing his rule over matters of life and death, and a globe in his left hand, symbolizing the totality of his reign. He wears a jeweled crown and appears impassive.

The Hierophant

This card may also be called the Pope in older or historically inspired decks, or the High Priest, as a counterpart to the High Priestess. The Hierophant is the bridge between deities and mortals, as well as the key to divine knowledge. He represents the importance or power of tradition, convention, and established institutions. Upright, this card can also symbolize guidance through some form of teacher and student relationship, whether this is in a spiritual, educational, creative, or domestic setting.

Finding this card in a spread may point the querent towards a conventional approach to their troubles, encouraging orthodoxy over radical or innovative choices. The Hierophant represents institutional knowledge and value structures, so he may appear to remind the querent of the tenets of their own morality.

Reversed - When the Hierophant is reversed, the querent may feel shackled, pinned down, or caged in by the rules of tradition. Perhaps the need to conform to social or religious norms is the only thing standing in the way of forward momentum for the sitter. This reversed card encourages rebellion, innovation, and rejection of institutional wisdom. Alternatively, the upturned Hierophant can indicate the need to question the teachings of a tutor, guru, or spiritual leader who wields great influence over the querent, advising skepticism and critical thinking. Advise the querent to feel emboldened to take risks, but always ensure they are thinking for themselves as they do so.

Symbolism - There is a great deal of religious imagery in this card; though it can represent the traditions of educational or professional institutions as well, its ties to spirituality are strong. Like the High Priestess, the Hierophant is seated between two pillars, one of which represents law while the other represents liberty. He has one arm raised in benediction, while he holds a triple cross in the opposite hand. The keys to heaven are at his feet, and two worshippers kneel before him, ready to receive his wisdom.

This card typically features a male Hierophant, even in modern feminist decks. Some decks may choose to omit any explicitly Christian religious symbols, while others may depict the Hierophant as the Pope in actuality.

The Lovers

This card may seem self-explanatory, but there is a lot more meaning to it than just romantic love. Love comes in many forms, whether familial, platonic, or romantic, and this card addresses them all. When the Lovers appear upright in a spread, they frequently represent a major choice, dichotomy, or a fork in the road, implying that whatever decision is made, the querent will have to sacrifice something in order to embrace their choice fully.

Reversed - Predictably, a reversal of this card can indicate that there is trouble brewing in the querent's relationships: lack of commitment, infidelity, indecisiveness, separation, or problems with trust. When the Lovers are reversed in a spread, it is often an indication that the querent needs to make a decision, or fully honor a choice they've already made.

Symbolism - In the Rider-Waite deck, the Lovers are drawn as Adam and Eve, standing naked in the Garden of Eden; their nudity is a representation of honesty and emotional vulnerability. Eve stands in front of the biblical Tree of Knowledge of Good and Evil, fruiting ripe apples with a snake coiled around its trunk. Adam stands before the Tree of Life. Above them is the Archangel Raphael, wings and arms spread wide, sun shining bright; Raphael's name means "God Heals," so this card references the power of love as a cure-all for emotional and physical ailments, and possibly equates the power of love to divine force.

Earlier decks most often depicted the Lovers as regular people, fully clothed, receiving a marriage blessing from a priest or other revered figure. The choice to illustrate this biblical scene in the Rider-Waite deck may have been meant to punctuate the sense of finality in whatever choice the querent must make; this card is not only indicative of an upcoming fork in the road but also of the fact that once one path is taken, there can be no turning back. In earlier times, when divorce was far less frequent and considered scandalous or even criminal, this card's illustration of a typical marriage was enough to reference this finality. The modern update to this biblical scene can be widely understood as a representation of temptation, innocence lost, and irreversible acts.

The Chariot

Following the Lovers in the Fool's journey, the Chariot card represents a commitment to the path chosen, no matter what challenges may arise. When this card appears in any spread, it often references a long and arduous journey, creative process, or project, but so long as the card is upright, the implication is that the hard work will all prove to be worthwhile in the end. Success can be found through focus, hard work, and unwavering dedication to your chosen goals. There may be setbacks, hurdles, conflicts, and difficulties, but each problem encountered will be an important step in the journey, building strength of character and resilience. The Chariot references ambition and drive, focus, determination, and endurance. It embodies the spirit of a person who refuses to accept defeat and sees victory and success as imperative, not optional.

Reversed - When this card appears upturned in a spread, it's a clear sign that the querent's current plan or path is not going to take them where they're hoping to go. The problem might be momentum; perhaps the sitter is moving too slowly, too quickly, trying to run before they've learned to walk, or wasting time on overtraining, making the perfect the enemy of the good. The reversed Chariot can also be a sign that the querent has lost sight of their goals, become distracted or disempowered, or encountered a roadblock that they cannot find a way around. Whatever the context, this card advises you to stop, turn around, and find another route; the current path won't lead anywhere good.

Symbolism - This card features a figure wearing a crown or helmet, standing triumphant upon a chariot, ushered forward by Egyptian sphinxes or horses. The sphinxes or horses are white and black, symbolizing the balance of good and bad encountered in his journey. In some decks, the crowned figure also has wings. He wears a suit of armor adorned with crescent moons, and above him is a canopy decorated with a celestial pattern; these two elements represent divine protection. He doesn't hold any reigns; instead, he seems to steer his steeds with the scepter in his right hand, and through the sheer power of his will. A river flows behind the scene, representing motion and change, as well as the futility of swimming against the current.

Strength

Historically, this card has also been called "Fortitude," and in some modern occult decks, it was renamed "Lust." No matter the era, this card references a form of inner strength, rather than the purely physical power that is depicted in the Chariot card. It references courage, persuasive power or influence, patience, and emotional resilience. When appearing in a spread, this card may serve to remind the sitter that strength can be sensitive, sweet, and silent; that problems can be resolved without conflict, and situations can be controlled without the use of excessive force. It may symbolize intellectual prowess, diplomatic skill, stamina or persistence.

Reversed - This signifies a lack of emotional strength: cowardice, self-doubt, misplaced anger, and overindulgent behaviors have weakened the querent. They may be struggling with self-control, or failing to take responsibility for their actions, and feeling stagnant or stuck in a rut as a result of these problems. The reversed Strength card is a call to restore inner-balance, atone for past wrongs, and find healthier methods of channeling negative emotions. While upright, the Strength card can symbolize the power that is found through taming inner demons; in reverse, though, it may mean that the querent's inner darkness has been allowed to spiral out of control, and needs treatment.

Alternatively, the reversed Strength card could indicate a misuse of inner strength. Is the sitter, or someone in their life, using their influence to coerce, manipulate, or exploit others?

Symbolism - In the Rider-Waite deck, this card features a woman taming a lion, hands placed gently over the beast's forehead and lower jaw. Like the Magician, this woman has an infinity symbol floating above her head, pointing to the limitless nature of emotional strength. The lion is a symbol of strength, courage, passion, and regal power; it also signifies the ego, or raw animal instinct, inside each and every one of us, which the female figure has easily under control. In many illustrations, she looks down towards the lion with concern, while the lion gazes up at her with admiration, sometimes licking her hands; it's clear that her power comes from sensitivity, and that she has earned the animal's respect and obedience through kindness. She wears a belt and garland made of roses, a symbol of victory and triumph.

In older decks, this illustration sometimes featured a woman breaking a stone pillar in half, referencing a form of strength through bravery, determination, and firmness.

The Hermit

Our modern conceptions of this title are often negative, but this card doesn't bear implicitly positive or negative connotations. The Hermit card is all about introspection, seeking guidance, and searching for truth. Sometimes, that denotes isolation, even long periods of total solitude, but this card doesn't always need to be interpreted to such an extreme degree. The Hermit can indicate that the querent needs to withdraw from something in their life in order to find what they need; for instance, pulling back from a friendship, club, or team that is distracting you or leading you to test the limits of your morals and values. Sometimes, the Hermit's isolation comes incidentally, as he embarks upon a quest to find spiritual guidance and must allow frivolous things to fall behind him. This card may symbolize the sacrifice of material possessions or institutional involvement. When it is upright, though, that usually means the life of sacrifice and isolation is undertaken willfully in pursuit of something greater, more important, than whatever the Hermit is leaving behind.

When upright in a spread, this card almost always encourages the querent towards meditation of some form. Even for the healthiest of minds and bodies, it is never a bad idea!

Reversed - When reversed, the Hermit can be a good sign, as it may mean a return or comeback, and an ending to the period of searching and solitude. Sometimes, though, it may signify a return to the same old story that the querent initially sought to escape; this may be a warning not to repeat the same mistake twice, or to end your quest before you've thoroughly learned your lesson. Alternatively, the reversed Hermit can represent isolation taken to an unhealthy extreme: antisocial or hostile behavior, fear of interactions or other people, and so on. It's very important to look to the context when you see this card reversed in a spread; it is an urgent call for the querent to rethink some aspects of their social life (or lack thereof), but it may not always be a dire warning. Perhaps it's simply an encouragement not to give up on a connection you considered letting go of.

Symbolism - The Hermit is cast as an old man with a long beard in hooded robes, trudging along through a barren landscape. He uses a walking staff, and lights his way forward with a lantern that contains a six-pointed star, which is divine light; still, he stares at the ground. Every aspect of this illustration holds meaning. The Hermit's lantern is actually the Lamp of Truth, a guiding light for the lost soul, and his walking stick is the Patriarch's Staff, a symbol of authority and enlightenment. He is alone, and in his cloak, he is hiding from humanity; yet, he is on the move, searching for something.

Wheel of Fortune

This card is all about cyclical change. It references the circle of life, karmic rewards, and turning the tables. Something in the querent's life is about to change, or very recently has changed, and the results will involve poetic ironies, role reversals, and changes in station. It very often refers to a change in material wealth or power status. Upright, it can be a symbol of good luck or an upcoming fortuitous turn of events in the querent's life. It can just as easily be a symbol that change is constant, and nothing good can last forever; if the querent has had a recent streak of good fortune, this card might be a warning not to get too comfortable floating up there on cloud nine.

Reversed - This may be a sign that bad luck is just around the corner. It could also point to an unexpected change of fate or the possibility of a sudden loss being followed by a greater gain. A reversed Wheel of Fortune card depends on context for precise interpretation, but it certainly never encourages the querent to take any unnecessary risks or major gambles in the near future.

Symbolism - In this card, we see a revolving wheel filled with letters and symbols; the letters spell out "T-A-R-O" and in between each of these are the letters "Y-H-W-H" meaning God of Israel. A sphinx sits atop the wheel, sword in hand, representing the well-guarded mysteries of fate and chance. A snake slithers along another arc of the circle, symbolizing growth and transformation, shedding skin that no longer fits. On the underside of the circle is Anubis, an Egyptian God associated with death and the afterlife, rising with the upward turn of the wheel, representing the start of a new cycle of life. In each of the four corners of the card is a winged figure with an open book: an angel, a griffin, a horned bull, and a lion. These figures correlate to the four elements (air, fire, water, and earth), as well as the four suits of the Tarot deck, and the four fixed signs of the zodiac calendar (Aquarius, Scorpio, Taurus, and Leo).

Justice

The name says it all. This card is about justice prevailing, restoring karmic balance and equilibrium. It also implies truth surfacing, virtues upheld, debts paid and promises honored. The Justice card promises a fair resolution to the querent's concerns; alternatively, it may indicate that Justice is coming to seek what the sitter owes to it. The querent will be taught the value of responsibility, accountability, and the golden rule of treating others as you wish to be treated. This card urges the querent to look at the patterns of cause and effect within their life and to behave with integrity and honor moving forward.

Reversed - This represents a literal inversion or corruption of justice: unfair rulings, institutional bias, false testimony, rigged outcomes, misplaced blame and dodged karmic punishments are all possibilities for the querent's future. This reversed card may be a warning to the sitter to do the right thing, own up to past mistakes, honor promises made, and face the consequences of their actions head on. It can also be a warning that other characters in the querent's life will fail to meet these standards of integrity and righteousness when it matters most.

Symbolism - The Justice card depicts a figure--usually a woman, but sometimes an androgynous creature or male--either seated upon a throne like the Emperor or Hierophant, or standing, between two stone pillars, which symbolize the stable foundation of rationality and impartiality. The figure holds the sword of truth in one hand, pointed up towards the sky, and a set of golden scales in the other, hanging low at the figure's side. The scales may reference the Egyptian Goddesses Maat and Isis, who carried golden scales to symbolize justice and equilibrium.

The figure wears a jeweled crown in the Rider-Waite deck and many others; sometimes, instead of a crown, the figure wears nothing upon its head except for a blindfold, a reference to the common artistic depictions of Lady Justice, or Justitia, that became popularized throughout Europe in the 1600s.

The Hanged Man

This card's title may have given it a bad reputation that it never deserved to carry. The Hanged Man may sound like a negative card, but facing upright, it actually has a lot of positivity to offer to the sitter in certain contexts. To put it simply, this card is all about letting go; that being said, there's hardly anything simple about that concept, nor is there an easy one-size-fits-all interpretation for the Hanged Man card within a spread. Sometimes, he can symbolize sacrifice; sometimes, surrender; other times, it may mean a suspension of time or lack of momentum. Usually, though, these things can be seen in a positive light if the card is upright, and the Hanged Man character is hanging upside down. This card points to sacrifices made willingly, voluntary atonement, a shedding of the ego, and acceptance of divine will. It can also refer to emotional vulnerability; giving in to a difficult experience in order to get the most out of it, or even enjoy it; living in the moment; staying patient, knowing better opportunities will come to those who can wait; complete and utter devotion to a spiritual faith; or release of a struggle or conflict that has caused the querent emotional stress. This card can symbolize forgiveness, and the wisdom that comes from knowing that acceptance and surrender are signs of strength, not weakness.

Reversed - When the Hanged Man is flipped in a spread, it points to a character who is unable to let go. This might be the sitter or someone who plays an important role in their life; either way, this person may be struggling to set aside the ego, to release their grip on someone or something under their control, or to give up an old grudge. It can also represent sacrifices made in vain, or time wasted on fruitless efforts.

Symbolism - The Hanged Man is strung up by one of his ankles, not his neck, hanging upside down from a tree branch. The tree may symbolize the World Tree of Norse mythology, also called Yggdrasil, which Odin hung himself upon, stabbing himself and refusing the help of other Gods, offering his own blood as a sacrifice in order to learn the runes that control the heavenly and mortal realms; it is also drawn in the shape of a capital letter T in the Rider-Waite deck, perhaps also referencing the biblical cross upon which Jesus was sacrificed.

In most decks, the Hanged Man wears a serene expression, or sometimes even smiles, even in historical decks from time periods in which this form of torture was actually used to punish traitors. This shows us that he accepts his vulnerable position; perhaps he even thought it for himself on purpose. His head is usually surrounded by a halo or aura of light, which symbolizes spiritual wisdom or philosophical enlightenment. His free leg is bent at a right angle and crossed behind his suspended knee; this represents a crossroads, and it draws the shape of the number four, perhaps referencing the four corners (north, south, east and west), four seasons, or four suits of the deck.

Death

This is perhaps the most widely misunderstood card in the entire Tarot deck. Its title is certainly foreboding, and considering the fact that most decks use the imagery of a skeletal figure riding horseback as one of the harbingers of the apocalypse, it's no wonder this card is feared. But in truth, the Death card rarely implies any sort of literal, physical death, and the kinds of death it does foretell of can often be good for the querent. For instance, the death of a cancerous tumor the sitter has been fighting off, or the death of a relationship that was holding them down rather than lifting them up. This card speaks of destruction and creation, resolutions and new beginnings.

The Death card also has a strong connection to the concept of rebirth. It does not simply remind us that all things eventually come to an end--it serves to remind us that death makes way for new life, and endings lead to new beginnings. It ultimately symbolizes change--usually drastic and permanent change. Look strongly into the context and surrounding cards before interpreting this card as a negative sign in any reading. It means that something big is coming, but first, something has to be lost or destroyed to make space for it. This isn't always a bad thing.

Reversed - When you find this card in reverse, the sitter is likely trying to resist necessary changes in their life or feeling stuck. It can represent procrastination, lack of progress or momentum, or the inability to resolve something that is dragging on and on, draining the sitter's mental and physical energy. It can also indicate that the querent (or someone important in their life) is digging their heels into the sand and refusing to be moved, despite the signs that a storm is coming and the tide is rising.

Symbolism - In the Rider-Waite deck, this card portrays a skeletal figure in either a suit of armor or a dark cloak riding upon a white horse, stepping over what appears to be a deceased king, his crown having fallen off and into the dirt as he fell dead. The color of the horse signifies purity, and the animal itself symbolizes forward movement; the steed is a symbol of purification as an element of progress and change. The skeletal rider carries a black flag with a white rose and the number thirteen in roman numerals; coincidentally, a child kneeling before the horse also offers up a bouquet of white roses to the rider. The white rose is also a symbol of purity, transformation, and hope; the fact that the youngest child on the card holds it references the idea of rebirth, and reminds us to stay optimistic for the future, despite the fears the rider may stir up within us all.

The dead king serves to remind us that death and change are great equalizers--no one is exempt from these experiences, no matter their status. The other figures in the scene represent different manners in which people handle change. The pope stands and appears to be praying or maybe pleading for mercy. The wreathed maiden kneels and turns her head away, perhaps afraid, or in denial. The childbearing the bouquet smiles up at the rider as if to welcome him.

In the background, there is a wasteland dotted with grave markers; a pond, and further beyond that, a river with a ship sailing on it. Far in the distance, between two great stone towers, the sun is rising; a new day is dawning.

In many earlier decks, the Death card depicts a much simpler scene: the grim reaper stands with no white horse in sight, and is often bare-boned, without armor or a flag, holding only a scythe. In those decks, he might have been surrounded by dead figures from all classes and walks of life, or he might have stood alone. Historically, this card might have been left unlabeled, for superstitious reasons, and referred to verbally as the "the card with no name." In many modern decks, the card is named "Death-Rebirth," or simply "Rebirth."

Temperance

This card serves to remind us of the importance of balance. When facing upright, it references moderation, sobriety, and healing. It also signifies patience, emotional strength, self-control, stability, routine, and spiritual faith. The Temperance card urges the sitter to maintain a sense of calm, even in the midst of chaotic change.

This card features some alchemical imagery as well; it symbolizes blending, experimenting, mixing elements in unusual combinations. Temperance suggests that most things can be good in moderation, but it may take the querent a period of trial-and-error to find their perfect balance.

Reversed - Some elements of the querent's life is out of balance, and pretty soon, the consequences are going to start catching up with them in a big way. This reversed card is a sign that one or more of the sitter's vices has begun to spiral out of control. It could reference a habit like smoking, excessive drinking, or overeating, but it could also reference a relationship that has grown far too intimate in a very short period of time or a job that has taken over the sitter's life and overtaken their other values. When reversed, Temperance urges the querent to take a sharp critical eye to their own behaviors and trim those that may be causing them harm. Addictions need to be recognized and managed; exposure to toxic relationships should be minimized; risky behaviors should be avoided by a wide mile, at least for the time being. Curb overindulgence, and aim to restore calm and balance.

Symbolism - This card depicts an angel standing by a river bank, pouring water between two chalices, wings spread wide. She wears robes of white or light blue, with an upward pointing triangle encapsulated by a square on the front of it; this symbolizes the notion that mortals are bound by the laws of earth and science. The triangle is also recognized as a symbol of healing. She stands with one foot dipped in the river, and one foot firmly planted on the riverbank; this symbolizes the concept of testing the waters before diving in, as well as the idea that we are all connections between disparate elements, and can act as harbingers of peace and harmony.

The water poured between cups references the art of alchemy, making something greater than the sum of its parts through hard work, dedicated focus, and a little divine guidance. Beside the angel is a path leading away from the riverbank towards what looks like a rising sun, but is actually a golden crown; this symbolizes the journey or experience that leads the angel to this state of peace and serenity, as well as the lengthy process of attaining mastery over the alchemical arts, as well as over internal balance.

In the Thoth deck and others inspired by it, this card is renamed "Art."

The Devil

Another card that is often misunderstood is the Devil. This card doesn't necessarily imply that something evil or nefarious is underfoot. Instead, it references a feeling of entrapment. It might symbolize an addiction or bad habit, like substance abuse or gambling; it could also point to a dangerous relationship, work environment, institution or community that the querent feels unable to leave behind, even though they recognize the harm it is causing them. The sitter feels powerless in the face of temptation, and cannot help themselves to stop. The upright Devil card may reference feelings of enslavement to material wealth, power or status symbols; succumbing to dangerous temptation and exhibiting lustful behaviors; enabling domination, bondage or manipulation; and serving only the physical body, to the detriment of the mind and spirit.

Reversed - When this card is reversed, the querent is ready to break free of whatever addiction, habit, or relationship is holding them back. This is easier said than done, though. The Devil's entrapment isn't purely forceful; his slaves are with him because, on some level, they want to be there. The sitter must be prepared to face their own inner demons in order to sever ties with the sources of negativity that are dragging them down, and get ready for a challenging journey.

The reversed Devil can also symbolize detachment; this may mean detachment from material possessions, from the physical sensations of the body, from painful emotion, or physical detachment from a place or person who is limiting you. This card urges the sitter to cut the cord, break the chain, quit the habit, and work to restore control and independence.

Symbolism - In the Rider-Waite deck, the Devil is portrayed as Baphomet (or the Horned Goat of Mendes), a satyr with furry legs, harpy talons in place of hooves, a goat's head and horns atop a man's torso, and enormous bat wings sprouting from his back. He also bears an inverted pentagram on his forehead between his horns, in the place where a crown might rest. The reversed five-pointed star is a mark of black magic, or the Left-Hand Path, which is not necessarily equated with evil; Baphomet is actually a deity of binary dichotomies, like good and evil, masculine and feminine, birth and death, and so on, so his demonic appearance shouldn't be mistaken for pure monstrosity. He holds one hand up in blessing, while the opposite hand hangs low, holding an upended torch, flames pointing towards the ground.

Baphomet is perched upon a pedestal; chained to the pedestal is a woman and a man, both naked with their hands-free. The man has a tail of fire, while the woman has a tail of red grapes, symbols of passion and lust, respectively. They wear the chains loosely around their necks, perhaps implying that they aren't exactly being held against their wills; both are sprouting horns of their own, showing that the more time they spend in the Devil's presence, the more they are inclined to adopt his traits.

The Tower

The Tower card is all about chaos, upheaval, and cataclysmic change. It's another card that looks immediately foreboding and has earned itself a bad reputation, but it isn't always a bad sign within a spread. In some contexts, the upright card can signify danger or destruction, but it can also reference positive change coming in the form of a revolution, or a happy accident. It can point to oncoming storms, both literal and figurative, but it can also symbolize liberation, and the freedom to rebuild upon a stronger, superior foundation to the one that has crumbled. The key to this card is that it implies a sudden disruption of the status quo, rather than a gradual shift or transformation. It also implies that the change will be unforeseen, either coming out of left field or, if it is somewhat anticipated, arriving earlier or with more violent force than expected.

Reversed - When the Tower is reversed, the sitter can still expect change in the near future; in this case, though, the change may be subtle, gentle, slow and steady, rather than chaotic and explosive. Alternatively, if appearing in a spread after a personal question or prompt, the reversed Tower card might indicate a reluctance to accept change or a period of great personal growth and inner turmoil. For example, a devout religious person experiencing a crisis of faith could turn up the reversed Tower in a spread; likewise, this card could be drawn for someone going through an existential crisis, or losing interest in a career field that they've been dedicating their lives to for years. If a querent is questioning their purpose or the meaning of their life, the reversed Tower urges them to embrace change. Out with the old, and in with the new.

Symbolism - We see a tall and narrow grey building, built upon a narrow mountainous ridge, being struck by a lightning bolt, which represents insight, epiphany, and a surge of new energy. The mountain's small size in comparison to the grand height of the Tower is significant; the tall building represents lofty ambitions or enormous promises built upon falsities and exaggerations. The few windows the Tower has are spewing flames, and people are tumbling out of them, falling face first towards the ground, presumably having leaped to their deaths. They represent the concept of losing control, being backed into a corner or stuck between a rock and a hard place, forced to make a decision you might never otherwise make. At the top of the tower is a large crown--large enough to function as the roof of the building--that is being blasted off of the building by the lightning bolt. This represents the dismantling of the ego through opening of the crown chakra. There are twenty-two balls of flame in the sky behind the falling figures; these represent the twelve zodiac signs and the ten nodes of the tree of life, symbolizing the fact that divine balance is constant, even in the face of catastrophic tumult.

The Star

The upright Star card represents a sliver of hope that leads you through to the other side of disaster--the calm and peace that comes after the storm is over, or the miracle that restores your faith, even if it seemed for a moment as though all might be lost. It signifies belief and optimism, inspiration, personal reinvention, and unwavering trust in divine guidance. It points to blessings, opportunities, and good luck, and a sense of cosmic importance or divine purpose.

Reversed - The reversed Star card symbolizes cynicism, negativity, closed-mindedness, or stagnation. It can indicate a loss of hope, a sense of being overwhelmed by every aspect of life, or tested convictions. The sitter who receives a reversed Star may be in dire need of an attitude adjustment or lifestyle change, lest the universe return all the negativity in their outlook by tenfold. When this card is upside down, it can also point to a health problem or hidden injury left over from a disastrous event, preventing the querent from truly moving past it. It may also imply that the querent is struggling with symptoms of depression, such as lack of interest in things they once enjoyed, a pessimistic outlook, the desire to disengage from social engagements or other activities, and so on. The querent must do whatever it takes to turn their gaze back up to the celestial heavens and find a source of renewed hope.

Symbolism - Beneath a sky full of eight-pointed stars, a naked young woman kneels at the edge of a small pool. She holds two water jugs, pouring one jug of water back into the pool she upends the other over the grassy bank, nourishing the earth. She pours these freely, as though the jugs will never run empty; this signifies the abundance of the universe and free-flowing energy. The jug in her right hand is stretched out in front of her, pouring into the water, representing the conscious mind, while the jug in her left-hand pours out behind her back, representing the subconscious, and diverging into five rivulets on the ground, each standing for one of the five senses. Much like the angel on the Temperance card, the young woman kneels with one foot submerged in the water, while the other foot remains on dry land; this stance symbolizes her inner balance, rooted in intuition and rationality, emotion and practicality, esoteric and scientific knowledge.

Behind the young woman is a tree upon a shallow hill, with one lone ibis bird perched atop it, a symbol of creativity and aspiration. Above her are eight stars in total, one of which shines larger and brighter than all the rest, representing her core identity. The other seven smaller stars represent each of the chakras. The woman's nudity is a symbol of her vulnerability; she is ready to surrender herself to divine will.

The Moon

In the Rider-Waite deck, this card has a deceptively optimistic color scheme. In Tarot, the Moon card symbolizes fear of the unknown, subconscious memory, suspicion, dishonesty, an illusion. The Moon implies fluctuation, uncertainty, miscommunication and a lack of clarity. Someone in the querent's life is not who they appear to be; some situation or circumstance is only half understood; something is in flux and cannot be grasped by the sitter, at least not for the time being. Perhaps someone is keeping a secret that could change the querent's perspective entirely, or someone holds hidden ulterior motives. This card encourages the querent to rely on their intuition because their extrasensory perceptions cannot be trusted. Furthermore, it urges the querent to release negativity and painful memories that may be clouding their judgment of the current situation.

The Moon is cyclical; this card can represent repressed memories or emotions returning, old fears resurfacing, and recurring dreams or nightmares. It has a strong feminine energy, but that should be thought of in terms of feminine characteristics or traits only--it may not reference an actual woman.

Reversed - When the Moon card is reversed, a bright, clear light is shone upon that which used to mystify the sitter. Secrets are unveiled, disguises lifted, and illusions dissolved. This doesn't always lead to happiness, though; the reversed Moon can point to sadness and confusion, especially in the context of retrieving difficult memories or exposing painful secrets. Generally speaking, though, the reversed Moon is a sign that a fog is lifting; anxiety is ready to be released, fears will soon be overcome, and challenges will be conquered. The querent may be on the verge of an awakening, or a new stage of enlightenment.

Symbolism - This card's illustration is full of dualities. The Moon itself appears as both a crescent and a full sphere; the sphere is bright and looks almost as if it could be the sun. The Moon hangs in the sky between two distant towers, symbolizing the choice between right and wrong, good and evil; the towers look exactly the same. In the foreground lies the edge of a body of water, presumably the ocean, out of which a large crayfish is emerging; he represents hidden fears, suppressed emotions, and repressed memories coming resurfacing from the murky depths of the subconscious. There is a path leading from the shoreline to a mountain range in the distance, running between the two towers. On either side of it is a domestic dog barking at the moon, and a wild wolf howling. These creatures reference someone's animal instincts, or their wild, dark side. When we walk the path below the Moon, we are on a tightrope between the known and unknown, the conscious and subconscious, the domesticated and the wild, the present and the past, the natural and the supernatural.

The Sun

The warm and positive energy of this card is usually obvious, even in esoteric decks. The Sun means good fortune, joy, blessings, achievement, and fulfillment. If the querent has brought a problem or complex question to the reading, this upright card points to positive resolutions, and outcomes exceeding expectations. It encourages the sitter to move forward with confidence and self-assurance. Let yourself be radiant; it is your turn to bask in the sunlight.

Reversed - When the Sun is reversed, it doesn't simply mean the opposite of the upright card; even upside down, this card never bears deeply negative connotations. Rather than implying true unhappiness, the reversed Sun points to clouded or muted joy. It often references doubt, dying enthusiasm, or unrealistic expectations overshadowing what should be a happy time. This is often a call to get in touch with your inner child. Perhaps the only thing muting your happiness is your inhibition, your ego, your stress or anxiety; what happens if you can let go of all that, and live in the moment, as a child would?

Symbolism - This illustration in the Rider-Waite deck is bright and busy, with a large anthropomorphized sun filling the top half of the card; below, a young naked child or baby rides a white horse before a grey rock wall, behind which a garden of sunflowers blooms. The grey wall symbolizes the hurdles or challenges overcome to reach this state of happiness. There are four sunflowers, representing the four elements or suits of the Minor Arcana; they represent optimism and emotional resilience. The child is a symbol of new beginnings; the baby's nudity represents freedom from negativity, worry, and doubt. The child holds a large red banner, a sign of announcement: changes are coming, and they will serve to feed the querent's sense of joy and satisfaction.

Judgment

This card points to a major reckoning. It is sometimes called "Resurrection," and it usually points toward a period of spiritual or philosophical awakening, reunion, rebirth, and absolution. It can also indicate homesickness, forgiveness, and a renewal of faith or belief. Finally, it may come up in the context of certain spreads to warn the sitter that karmic retribution is coming and that they would be wise to practice some self-evaluation and prepare to receive their own karmic rewards or punishments.

The Judgement card indicates that the querent is faced with major decisions or choices and that if they are able to choose wisely and thoughtfully, the choice they make will lead them to a higher level of consciousness, emotional health, and spiritual growth.

Much like the Tower, this card represents change, transition, and new beginnings; however, with the upright Judgement card in a spread, the querent can most likely expect a gradual or peaceful transition, rather than change heralded by a cataclysmic event.

This card may also indicate that the change is not inspired by any single external event, but rather found through introspection, observation and rational thought—or perhaps an unexplained inner calling. It may reference long term plans finally coming to fruition or dreams realized at long last.

The Judgement card encourages the querent to self-reflect, and choose their next steps through logical thought or spiritual guidance, rather than mere intuition.

Reversed - If you've ever known, either in your gut or your bones, that the universe was trying to tell you something, but you decidedly ignored the message, then you understand the energy of this reversed card. When the Judgement card appears upside down within a spread, it can often indicate that something is clouding the querent's ability to judge themselves or their circumstances rationally or fairly. It references self-doubt, emotional dishonesty, refusal to accept blame, a poor or distorted sense of self-awareness, stubbornness, and denial. The querent may be unable to engage in meaningful self-reflection due to the impulse to project, judging others too harshly while avoiding the gaze of the mirror. It may also point towards a person who has been dodging their karmic justice for a long time and won't be able to outrun it much longer.

Symbolism - From the blue skies above, the archangel Gabriel, a messenger of God, emerges from the clouds, blowing his trumpet down towards the earth. His wings are spread wide and his face is serene; his judgment is neither malicious nor unduly merciful. There is a flag tied to the trumpet, white with a red cross; this is a symbolic reference to a crossroads, either physical, mental, or emotional. Meanwhile, the horn is a wake-up call, announcement, or divine message.

Below the archangel, a group of people stand nude, gazing upwards with their arms outstretched and open, ready to receive and embrace Gabriel's message. Their nudity represents purity, innocence, and honesty; they are ready for Judgement. Many of these people are emerging from coffins: this does not literally represent resurrection from death, but rather the idea of leaving behind the aspects of a life that kept the querent feeling caged in, limited, or stuck.

The World

The final card of the Major Arcana represents the culmination, or ultimate destination, of the Fool's journey; by now, he has taken advice from many teachers, experimented with masculine and feminine energy, isolation and gregariousness, creation and destruction, patience and rapid change. He has embraced all of life's lessons and now feels at one with the universe. His journey of awakening and enlightenment may not be fully complete, but he is no longer a Fool--he is ready to become a teacher himself.

When the World appears upright in a spread, it is almost always a good sign. It signifies completion, success, accomplishment, and well-earned rewards. The sitter is approaching or has already reached spiritual nirvana. Things have come full circle, and they now have the perspective they need to handle the twists and turns of life with grace and contentment. It also indicates that the querent has reached a state of emotional stability and is now capable of true self-love. Finally, this card is a symbol of the cycle of life, reminding us that in order to become one with the divine, we must be able to give as well as receive and embrace endings as well as new beginnings.

Reversed - When this card is turned upside down, it signifies a lack of closure or completion. Something in the querent's life remains unresolved, and it is causing stagnation and internal blockage, preventing them from exhaling or releasing. It may indicate that the sitter's plans, no matter how well they've been laid out, are not progressing as they should, and will not lead them to achieve their goals. It warns the sitter not to start counting their chickens before the eggs have hatched. It also warns against expecting to reach the finish line anytime soon if the querent has taken too many shortcuts in the past.

Symbolism - In the center of this card, a nude woman appears to be dancing or frolicking, as she hovers in a clear blue sky, her figure framed by a green laurel wreath, adorned with red ribbon. The laurel wreath represents triumph and achievement, as it was once awarded to victors of chariot races and other ancient sporting events. The woman holds a wand in each hand, a symbol of her powers of manifestation. She also has a purple cloth draped gently across her torso and pelvis, fluttering behind her in the wind; the color represents regality, loyalty, dedication, and constancy, reminding us that she reached this state of enlightenment through dogged pursuit, consistent effort, focus and unwavering faith. Her legs are crossed in a mirrored reflection of the Hanged Man's stance, signifying a crossroads once again, but this time it has been found through a state of empowerment; the woman knows she can make the most of whichever path she chooses next.

In the four corners of the card, we see the same creatures that adorn the corners of the Wheel of Fortune card: an angel, a griffin, a horned bull, and a lion, this time is illustrated in closeup. These figures signify a balance of the four elements and four seasons of the Zodiac: the angel represents the house of Aquarius, and air; the griffin represents Scorpio, and water; the bull represents Taurus, and earth; and the lion represents Leo, as well as fire. Interestingly, these are the same four creatures described in the Bible's Book of Revelations, surrounding the throne of God. They also represent the four suits of the Tarot deck, the four seasons, and the four corners of the earth.

CHAPTER 5
Beginning The Minor Arcana

It can certainly be tempting to spend all your time studying the Major Arcana cards, but seeing as they are vastly outnumbered by the suit cards in the deck, collectively referred to as the Minor Arcana, the chances that you'll encounter suit cards in any spread is quite high. Within the context of a spread, the cards of the Major Arcana can be weighed more heavily, or viewed as more important to the ultimate interpretation; you might think of them as major plot points within a story, whereas the cards of the Minor Arcana make up sub-plots and contextual histories. Still, the Minor Arcana cards cannot be ignored or disregarded; they help to translate the meanings of the Major Arcana cards from generalized concepts to useful and specific advice for the querent.

Luckily, there are some tricks you can use to decipher the meanings of the fifty-six cards in the Minor Arcana that will spare you the trouble of having to memorize each and every one. Regardless of the deck's style, whether it includes unique illustrations or simply abstract designs, each card in the Minor Arcana will have a suit and number. The suit's each correspond with an element, and the numbers all bear their own significance. By combining them, even novices can make some sense out of a suit card without having any preconceived notion of its meaning.

The Suits

The four suits of the Minor Arcana are Cups, Wands, Swords, and Pentacles. There are fourteen cards within each suit: an ace, two, three, four, five, six, seven, eight, nine and ten, as well as four Court Cards.

Bear in mind that the suits may be defined differently, especially in older decks. Historically, as tarot cards were used during the oppressive rule of the Roman Catholic church, which would not condone symbols of paganism, mysticism, or the occult, a suit of coins would be typically found in a tarot deck, in place of pentagrams, and you'd be much more likely to find a suit of staves, batons, or even polo clubs, rather than wands.

The Suit of Cups

All cards in this suit can be associated with the element of water. They largely correspond to our fluid emotions, feelings, and relationships.

The Suit of Wands

This suit is associated with the element of fire and represents action and passion, both creative and destructive in nature.

The Suit of Swords

These cards are correlated to the element of air and represent intangible ideas, truth, intellectual conflict, and physical, moral, or mental anguish.

The Suit of Pentacles

This suit is connected to the element of earth; having formerly been represented by coins in place of pentagrams, the cards concern practical matters such as finances, work, home, the body, and the essentials for living (sustenance, shelter, and safety).

How to Interpret Numbers in Suit Cards

It's important to remember that these meanings correlate to all of the numbers within the deck, not just the suit cards; these interpretations don't necessarily need to be applied to the cards of the Major Arcana, but with further study of numerology, Tarot readers can gain an even deeper understanding of all cards.

Furthermore, the direction of these cards and placement within a spread can impact meaning. For example, while a Four card would typically represent stability, if it is reversed, this might indicate just the opposite, and reference volatility or a weak foundation. Alternatively, if an upright Seven card usually represents a difficulty or challenge, a reversed Seven could indicate that something the querent expected to struggle with will actually turn out to be fairly easy.

Numbers

The Ace, or one, card means a new beginning or a fresh start. It may reference an opportunity, new relationship, or birth.

The Two card represents duality, division or union, choice, and dichotomy. It can point to relationship issues, forks in the road, mirror reflections, or repetition.

The Three card is related to creativity and growth. One obvious example of this is reproduction, or birth, turning a couple into a family; but this can also reference artistic creation, building, or personal development.

The Four card indicates stability, strength, and a steady foundation. It often references institutions, such as schools, churches, or even family units.

The Five card is about volatile change, conflict, or difficulty. Think of a person who feels like a fifth wheel on a double date; their presence creates tension in what would otherwise be a comfortable, stable, predictable situation.

The Six card means harmony, peace, balance, and contentment. It can also point to abundance, fulfillment, and satisfaction.

The Seven card signifies a challenge, hurdle, difficulty or struggle. As compared to the Five card, this signifies a problem that is more complex, without an easy solution. While the Five represents a state of discomfort that prompts change, the Seven refers to a lasting struggle that prompts introspection. It may help to think of Five as a representation of institutional problems, or group issues, while Seven references a problem that is personal to the querent.

The Eight card represents works come to fruition, manifestation, achievement, and accomplishment. It can also signify forward momentum, progress, and satiety. It is not only a representation of success and positivity, though; it can also point to situations that the querent once recognized as disasters waiting to happen, finally resulting in catastrophe, as expected.

The Nine card speaks to endings, both positive and negative; it can mean successful completion or devastation in the form of loss. Either way, it typically references an ending that leads to some form of isolation (in the Rider-Waite deck, every Nine card features an illustration of a solitary figure), heightened awareness of the self, and reliance on personal strength, wisdom, and resilience. It also tends to indicate a form of ending that leads to the anticipation of a new beginning or next chapter.

The Ten card also references endings, though it speaks to more permanent, conclusive endings than the Nine card. It can represent an ultimate manifestation or culmination of work, total completion, finality. It might help to think of the Nine card as representative of the negative or pessimistic side of an ending, while the Ten card represents positivity and optimism of a new beginning; see Nine as the grief of loss or death, while Ten holds the promise of rebirth. Alternatively, if the context of the spread rules out any negative interpretations of either card, you might look at the Nine as completion of a final test, or the last day of classes, while the Ten would reference a graduation ceremony, as well as the first step forward into the next chapter of life. Finally, remember that Nine cards always feature solitary figures, while Ten cards often portray couples or groups; the Nine is an ending that leads to solitude, while the Ten is an ending that calls for a celebratory party.

Combining suit and number for a formulaic interpretation

Novice cartomancers can get a rough feel for the meanings of numbered suit cards by combining the significance of the card's suit and number. Let's try a few examples below.

Two of Cups - The number represents duality, union or division, and choice. The suit references emotion and love. Layered together, these elements point toward a loving relationship or strong emotional connection between two people. The context of the spread and the querent's prompt will help the reader to discern whether these references a romantic, platonic, familial, or professional connection. If the card is facing upright, it will likely denote some positive development in the relationship; if reversed, this card may imply a division, conflict, or split.

Four of Swords - The number represents stability and fortitude. The suit is associated with intellect and conflict. Combining these notions, we can see that the card signifies intellectual strength or mental stability, possibly in the face of a challenge or hardship. The true meaning of the card takes this interpretation a step further; by reading the illustration of the card, which portrays a figure laid to rest in what appears to be a church, we can discern that this card points to an extended period of thought and introspection that is involuntary, probably prompted by physical incapacitation. This is precisely why novices will be able to learn more from illustrated decks like Rider-Waite Tarot, rather than a deck that uses abstract designs for the numbered suit cards.

Seven of Wands - The number signifies strife and hardship, while the suit implies passionate action, and creative energy. When we put these two concepts together, we can see this card represents an individual who is rolling up their sleeves to tackle a problem, ready to think outside of the box to find a solution, prepared to work hard to fix whatever is broken. It may also imply courage under fire.

Nine of Pentacles, and Ten of Pentacles - The numbers both represent completion in a sense; the Nine references an ending for the individual, while the Ten represents the total culmination of efforts. The suit, in this case, symbolizes practical matters, finances, physical health, and values. So we might then discern that the Nine of Pentacles symbolizes a person who has finally earned enough money to afford a vacation, retreat, or day of self-care; meanwhile, we could interpret the Ten of Pentacles card as a representative of a jackpot or windfall, company bonus or lottery winning. The Nine of Pentacles points to an individual who is pausing to enjoy the fruits of their labors, while the Ten of Pentacles points to a collective accomplishment that results in abundant rewards for all parties involved. Once again, the illustrations of these cards help to clarify the distinction.

The Court Cards

The specific titles of court cards can vary greatly from one deck to the next. The Rider-Waite deck includes a Page, Knight, Queen and King for each of the four suits, but by contrast, Crowley's Book of Thoth deck recasts them as a Princess, Prince, Queen, and Knight, in respective order of status. The Page is sometimes referred to as the Knave in older historical decks. Many modern decks aim to use gender-neutral titles for these cards or to invert traditional gender norms by making the Queen the highest status card, for example, or replacing all four characters with female titles. Regardless of their titles and genders, though, each Court Card is meant to represent a certain archetypal character, or personality type, that exists within the querent's life.

There are several different ways to read the Court Cards, which is where the personality, experience level, and intuitive gift of the reader factor into the interpretation of any spread. Many experienced cartomancers agree that the Court Cards usually represent specific people in the querent's life or archetypal characters. Interestingly, there are sixteen Court Cards in the Tarot deck, and they appear to roughly correspond to the sixteen different Myers-Briggs Personality Trait Indicator (or MBTI) types--though this is hardly an exact science, and opinions on card-MBTI connections vary.

While the Court Cards are typically drawn as detailed characters with distinctive features, it helps to bear in mind that they represent types of personalities, which can come in almost any physical form. A Queen of Cups card could easily represent a man, just as the King of Swords could denote a female in the querent's life.

Perhaps the easiest way to develop an understanding of the Court Cards is to think of them as formulaic combinations; they are each defined by their suit's element, their rank or status, and their masculine or feminine energy.

The four suits correspond to the four elements: swords to air, cups to water, fire to wands, and earth to pentacles or coins.

Each rank also corresponds to one of the four elements: Kings are linked to air, Queens to water, Knights to fire, and Pages to earth.

The elemental energy of air is control. A person ruled by the air element is usually clever, philosophical, and eccentric; carefree, optimistic, and charming; they may also be independent, selfish, and callous.

The elemental energy of water is understanding. A character ruled by water can be deeply emotional, compassionate, and intuitive; merciful, passive, and flexible; kind-hearted, introspective, and selfless to a fault; but also fickle, irrational, and deceptively powerful.

The elemental energy of fire is action. Someone ruled by the element of fire is typically bold, passionate, and charismatic; creative, adventurous, and courageous; lustful, irritable, and volatile; sometimes even violent and destructive.

The elemental energy of earth is acceptance. A person ruled by the earth element is usually practical, level-headed, and rational; emotionally stable, consistent, and responsible; respectful, humble, and sometimes a bit dull-spirited; open to learning and ready to do hard work to achieve end goals.

We can also correlate the Court Card ranks to their degree of maturity or experience. This is not a direct reference to literal age--the old can be quite childish, while the young can be wise beyond their years.

Additionally, we can link the masculine and feminine identities of the Court Cards to their yin and yang energies. The masculine Court Cards (Kings and Knights) can be thought of as active and assertive, while the feminine Court Cards (Queens and Pages, even if the Pages are drawn as men) can be considered passive and receptive.

Within the next few chapters, we'll discuss each specific Court Card's characteristics; for now, though, let's experiment with the formula of element + rank + gendered energy as an example of how to a novice might read a card that they are unfamiliar with, or haven't yet memorized.

Take the Page of Pentacles, for instance. The Page's rank correlates to the elemental energy of earth (practical, rational, eager to learn, accepting); his rank also implies that he is inexperienced, with a youthful spirit; finally, though he is portrayed in the Rider-Waite deck as a man, we can associate the rank of the Page with feminine energy, meaning he is passive and receptive. So without even knowing his suit, we can discern that this character is probably a hard worker, and due to his inexperience, a dedicated learner, open to receiving whatever wisdom the universe can offer him. Since his suit is Pentacles, or Coins, which often pertains to financial matters, we can look at the Page as a student or entrepreneur on the verge of success. He is a sign of good fortune soon to come, and he is able to receive it and put it to practical use.

Furthermore, you can deepen your understanding of the court cards by encapsulating the above formula within the suit element. For example, the King of Cups has elemental energy defined by his rank (King=air), a high level of maturity or experience, also due to his rank, and will tend to be assertive due to his gender. Typically, we might look at this formula and imagine a powerful person who is cocky, impulsive, perhaps even insensitive and selfish. But if we remember that this formula is also impacted by the suit element, we see that this personality exists within the context of water; this powerful, experienced, assertive personality is influenced by emotion, intuition, introspection, and passivity. The King of Cups can then be seen as a mature, authoritative, and bold person who has chosen to use his (or her) power for love, compassion, and selflessness.

These formulas can always be useful for cartomancers who prefer not to rely on strict memorization or rigid definitions of cards, as they leave a great deal of room for the reader to exercise their personal judgment and intuition. Nevertheless, we'll spend the next few chapters detailing the meanings of each numbered suit card and court card, so allowing both novices and experienced readers to perform effective readings with abstract historical and modern decks. When there are no illustrations to rely upon, readers may fail to grasp the nuance of their meanings, or easily lose track of the contextual implications that influence the card's interpretation.

CHAPTER 6
The Suit Of Cups

All cards within the Suit of Cups are correlated to the element of water, and reference emotion, love, relationships, compassion, and intuition. Both the Suit and its corresponding element are typically considered feminine, but this does not mean that these cards couldn't represent men or non-binary individuals.

In any spread, it's important to stay mindful of the fact that the cards of this suit reference feelings--they don't necessarily reflect behaviors or objective truth. As an example, a querent asking the Tarot deck for guidance in a romantic relationship might become dejected after receiving the Five of Cups and Seven of Cups, implying a change of heart and a conflict, as well as the reversed Two of Cups, implying a choice and division. Cumulatively, these cards point to a schism in the relationship. Perhaps a lover is tempted to stray from their partner in favor of a new love--that seems like the obvious interpretation, doesn't it?

At this point, though, the reader should recognize that these cards are all within the Suit of Cups, and may only signify feelings rather than actions. If none of the other cards within the spread support the idea of infidelity or a breakup in the near future, it's entirely possible that these cards are simply pointing out the querent's fear of losing their love to someone else. They may be warning against a self-fulfilling prophecy; if the querent fears adultery and allows this fear to impact their behavior, they may unwittingly end up driving their lover into the arms of someone else. Alternatively, these three Cup cards may explain that the querent's partner is physically committed to the current relationship, but struggling to integrate it with a change of heart in another walk of life: say, for instance, that the querent's partner wants to follow a job opportunity to a new home on the other side of the world, and doesn't know how to do this while maintaining the relationship. This story fits the three aforementioned cards just as well as a story of temptation and faithlessness.

Finally, depending on how many cards are included in your total spread, you may want to count up the number of cards laid from each suit. If the spread is overwhelmingly dominated by upright Cup cards, this can indicate that whatever the situation or prompt, the querent will need to connect deeply to their emotional body and trust in their intuition moving forward. It may also be a sign that the overall outcome will be determined by emotional reactions rather than rational thought or practical decisions. By contrast, if the spread is overwhelmed by reversed Cup cards, this might warn the querent that their emotions about the situation at hand will ultimately prove to be inconsequential, or that emotion is getting in the way of progress and resolution.

Always remember: context is key.

The Ace of Cups

Upright - A new emotional beginning; new love or a relationship progressing to another stage of intimacy; creativity.

Reversed - Emotional blockage or repression; unrequited love; creative stagnation.

Symbolism - This card shows a hand reaching out of a cloud, a symbol of divine gifts. A single cup rests in its upward facing palm, representing the Holy Grail--the ultimate symbol of love, devotion, and creativity. There is a dove above it, dropping a communion wafer into the chalice; the dove is a symbol of hope, peace, and healing, while the wafer references transformation. The hand and cup float above a pond with lotus flowers floating upon the water's surface; lotus flowers are a symbol of renewal, growth, and beauty.

Two of Cups

Upright - Mutual attraction; committed partnerships; strong love (romantic, platonic, or familial); stable union.

Reversed - Conflict; distrust; miscommunication; self-absorption; discord; schisms, splits, and breakups.

Symbolism - Two figures (a male and female) stand opposite one another; each holds a cup in one hand and reaches for the other with their free arm. Above them between the cups, is the Caduceus symbol, which references the staff of Hermes; it is also a modern symbol to represent western medicine, so it points to the healing powers of love. Above Caduceus is a winged lion's head, a representation of passion, courage, justice, and majesty.

Three of Cups

Upright - Joy and celebration; playfulness and creativity; gatherings and collaborations; "the more, the merrier" attitude; sharing happiness and spreading the love; supportive community.

Reversed - Overindulgence; hangovers, both literal and figurative; broken friendships and disjointed social circles; craving solitude.

Symbolism - Three women in bright colored robes dance together in a circle, each raising their cups high in the air. They wear floral wreaths, which denote victory and accomplishment. They are surrounded by grape vines, fruits, and a pumpkin, all of which represent a harvest, the reaping of rewards, and bountiful gifts from the divine.

Four of Cups

Upright - Solitude and introspection; emotional unavailability or withdrawal; apathy; disinterest; closed-mindedness; rejection.

Reversed - A comeback; seized opportunities; optimism, open-mindedness, and enthusiasm.

Symbolism - A young man sits at the base of a tree, arms crossed over his chest and eyes pointed towards the ground. You can tell by his body language that he is not open to giving or receiving love at this point in time. Before him, three cups are lined up and sit untouched, perhaps symbolizing that he has already emptied them, or that he has no interest in their contents. A fourth cup is offered to him by a phantom hand reaching through the clouds--a divine gift!--but he appears not to it.

Five of Cups

Upright - Melancholy; heartbreak; loss; regret; disappointment; anguish; sorrow; grief.

Reversed - Forgiving yourself; accepting losses; surrender; letting go of the past and moving on.

Symbolism - A solitary figure stands in a black mourning cloak, back turned towards us as he stares down at three spilled cups on the ground, either oblivious to the two upright cups behind him or willfully ignoring them. There is a castle in the distance, on the opposite side of a river, and a bridge leading there, symbolizing long-term goals, and the fact that this tragedy will eventually be a distant memory; in time, everything becomes water under the bridge.

Six of Cups

Upright - Childlike attitudes; pleasant strolls down memory lane; nostalgia and joy.

Reversed - Stuck in the past; holding grudges; rigidly following traditions with no room for playfulness, innovation, or experimentation.

Symbolism - Two children play in a garden beside a house; the older boy offers the younger girl a cup that holds a blooming flower. The house behind them represents stability, safety, and security. Behind them, a guard patrols the city, protecting them from external dangers and enabling their carefree playtime. The flowers symbolize youthfulness and growth.

Seven of Cups

Upright - Choices and decisions; wishful thinking; lofty ambitions; day-dreaming; abundant opportunities.

Reversed - Urgency of choice; if you do not pick one option soon, you may forfeit all of your opportunities.

Symbolism - A figure stands with his back to us; before him are seven cups, each spilling over with a different symbol: a face, which symbolizes either youth or love; a castle, symbolizing security and power; a wreath, representing victory; a snake, representing intrigue or temptation; a wyvern or dragon, standing for wrathful power; a pile of golden coins, symbolizing wealth and riches; and a shrouded figure with arms splayed wide, signifying spiritual enlightenment. These seven options may correlate to each of the seven deadly sins referenced in the bible.

Eight of Cups

Upright - Satiety, exhaustion, or boredom; walking away or moving on; abandonment, escapism, and wanderlust.

Reversed - A return; inability to let go; giving it one last shot; overstaying your welcome; biding time.

Symbolism - Eight cups are stacked upon a shoreline as a solitary figure ventures off, walking stick in hand, leaving the cups behind. The moon hangs overhead, a symbol of fluctuation and the cyclical nature of change. The figure seems to be heading towards mountains in the distance, implying that they are ready and eager to tackle challenges; change is often an uphill battle, but in this instance, difficulty is preferable to the sense of ease, comfort, and boredom being left behind.

Nine of Cups

Upright - Personal success and satisfaction; contentment; wealth and luxury; self-care; wishes fulfilled.

Reversed - Be careful what you wish for because you might get a whole lot of it; overindulgence; dissatisfaction; desire as a bottomless cup.

Symbolism - A man sits with his arms folded and a broad smile on his face; behind him, nine cups are lined up in a row upon an altar. His crossed arms show us that he has all needs and cannot receive anything more; his smile tells us that he is satisfied, and his feathered cap is a testament to his ambition, hard work, and well-deserved success.

Ten of Cups

Upright - The rewards you've waited your whole life for; true love; blessings; triumph; homecoming; joyful unions; alignment, coincidence, and synchronicity; bliss; spiritual fulfillment or nirvana.

Reversed - Missed connections; misalignment and misunderstandings; familial and romantic discord; deep social schisms. This can also reference the feeling of having everything you ever wanted, and still feeling incomplete or dissatisfied.

Symbolism - A family stands on a grassy plain beside a river, beneath a rainbow of cups. The mother and father each have one arm wrapped around their partner while the other arm reaches up towards the sky in gratitude and appreciation. The rainbow symbolizes glory, beauty, and divine blessings. The parents' collective stance displays both romantic and spiritual love. Beside them, their two children hold hands and dance joyfully, symbolizing innocence, hope, new beginnings, and the notion of coming full circle.

Page of Cups

Upright - The page is young and inexperienced, but deeply attuned to his emotions and intuitions. He is creative, curious, romantic, sensitive, naive and idealistic. He aims to spread the message of love, truth, and happiness. This card signifies new opportunities and new relationships.

Reversed - Hypersensitivity, immaturity, and refusal to be rational. This reversed card can also point to a failure to listen to or honor one's intuition.

Symbolism - The page stands with one hand on his hip; on the other hand, he holds a chalice with a fish peeking out over its brim. Much like the crayfish in the Moon card, this fish represents subconscious knowledge rising up from the murky depths and breaking the surface. Listen to your inner voice!

Knight of Cups

Upright - This character may have been the inspiration for the Prince Charming in your favorite fairy tale. He is romantic, noble, bold and valiant, and extremely charming. This card doesn't just reference love--it points to a romantic journey, or spiritual quest, as the Knight's rank is associated with active energy and inexperience. He's going places and winning plenty of hearts along the way.

Reversed - The reversed Knight of Cups calls to mind the feeling we get when something that once seemed too good to be true turns into a veritable nightmare. The Knight appears perfect and ideal on the outside, but just below the surface, there is jealousy, anger, moodiness, and emotional instability. This reversed card signifies a disconnection from reality or an illusion that masks an ugly truth.

Symbolism - The Knight rides a white horse, a symbol of the purity of his intention. He holds a cup up in offering. He wears a winged helmet, which references Mercury, a divine messenger; this indicates that he is silver-tongued, able to charm anyone with the beauty and eloquence of his communication style. He stares straight ahead, spine straight as a rod; he seems to know that he is being watched and admired.

Queen of Cups

Upright - This card represents the ultimate state of emotional balance. The Queen of Cups has been learning from her intuitive and emotional sensations for a lifetime. She is experienced now, an expert and authority on matters of the heart and soul. She is clairvoyant, creative, sensitive, emotionally mature, and a natural healer. Her compassion is like a beacon; others are drawn to her energy, inspired by her, comforted by her presence, and eager to accept her advice and guidance.

Reversed - Too much of a good thing can be really, really bad; emotion, intuition, and creativity are no exception. When this card is reversed, it implies that a potentially compassionate and emotionally mature person has instead become melodramatic, manipulative, obsessive, or dishonest. Most likely, they've lost touch with their empathetic drive, as their own extreme emotions and desires have grown to overshadow their perception of other people's needs and feelings. This can point to extreme narcissism disguised as love, or alternatively, to codependency.

Symbolism - The Queen sits on a throne at the edge of the sea. She wears a jeweled crown and holds an enormous and ornate cup, decorated with crosses, crescent moons, grapes, and other symbols; this represents spiritual wealth, or divine wisdom. She holds all the secrets of the universe in her palm. Her throne is decorated with seashells and cherubs who gaze upon her lovingly, with admiration. She is cradled both by the sea below and the heavens above.

King of Cups

Upright - This card combines the power of rationality with emotion and intuition. The King of Cups is a sign of love that has lasted the test of time, even after lust and novelty have faded away. He signifies commitment, compassion, generosity, benevolence, diplomacy, and peacemaking. He also stands for well-managed sensitivity; he feels things deeply, but never allows his emotions to overwhelm him or spur impulsive, volatile actions.

Reversed - Much like the reversed Queen of Cups, this card points to emotional instability and manipulation, but with a more forceful bent. The reversed King of Cups may be using coercion or emotional blackmail; he may be drowning in his addictions and unable to see through the fog of his emotions. He can also represent someone who fancies himself a powerful authority figure, blind to his own emotional immaturity and inconsiderate behavior.

Symbolism - The King sits upon his throne with a cup in one hand and a scepter in the other. He stares into the distance with a serene expression that implies emotional strength. He is alone, though, with his throne resting upon a platform floating in the sea; in the background, a ship passes in the distance, and a fish leaps from the water. The ship is a symbol of navigation, while the water symbolizes emotion and the subconscious. The leaping fish is representative of emotions and intuition rising to the surface. The grey stone platform upon which his throne sits symbolizes stability and fortitude.

CHAPTER 7
The Suit Of Wands

Wands aren't exclusively portrayed within this suit; like the other suit items (Cups, Wands, and Pentagrams) they show up in the Major Arcana illustrations as well, held by the Magician, and the princely warrior in the Chariot; the woman on the World card holds two!

In Tarot, Wands are symbols of manifestation, creation, passion, and action. They represent raw energy, ambition, determination, and transformation. The Suit of Wands is correlated to the element of fire, which, likewise, is a symbol of passion and energy, but also represents sexuality, volatility, expansion, release, and purification.

When a spread is dominated by the Suit of Wands, this is a sign that the querent should be focusing on turning possibilities into realities. Wands are the tools we use to project our thoughts and ideas into the external world, and when you encounter a large number of them in a Tarot spread, it's likely that the universe is calling you to step up to the plate and create something. The Wand is like a microphone and speaker box; this tool only amplifies and projects what is already inside of you, and your unique mind will manifest authentic creations with your unmistakable signature. What this means is that you do not need to be a creative type in order to heed the call of the Suit of Wands; you may create a business, create a family, or create a spiritual practice if these options make more sense to you than painting, writing, or dance. The point is innovation and invention--this suit is not necessarily geared toward artistic enterprise.

In esoteric Tarot decks, the Wand is connected to a mysterious energetic life force known as Qi, or Kundalini, in non-western metaphysical healing practices like Reiki and Chakra work in Tantra. This life force is a form of vitality that animates all living beings and drives them to fulfill their personal destinies. All the cards within this suit can be received as a call to action from the universe; this is not the time to rest on your laurels, or get caught up overthinking things. You are ready to solve problems, generate new ideas, bring people together, and put your plans in action. Set your sights on a goal, take hold of your wand, raise it high in the air, and manifest, manifest, manifest!

Ace of Wands

Upright - Ace cards generally represent new beginnings, and this card is no exception. This card denotes a new creative project or business venture; inspiration, invention, and opportunities that are just too good to pass up.

Reversed - This usually means that even if your latest project started out strong, it's falling flat, losing steam, or petering out. Distraction; procrastination; setbacks and delays; indecisiveness; poor planning.

Symbolism - A divine hand reaches out of the clouds holding up a wand that is sprouting leaves. Some of the leaves are falling down to the green earth below, where trees are growing--this symbolizes new possibilities, and seeds taking root. There is a river in the background, as well as a castle upon a distant hill. The river represents motion and momentum; the castle represents stability and security, but it is pretty far off, meaning that in order to create, you may have to embrace instability and get comfortable with vulnerability.

Two of Wands

Upright - Short term success; a first step in the right direction; planning and progress; discovery and achievement.

Reversed - Don't hesitate; if you act quickly, you can still seize this prime opportunity, but the moment will soon pass you by. This card can represent poor planning, self-doubt, fruitless anxiety, and fear of risk.

Symbolism - A cloaked man stands upon a balcony, holding a long Wand (technically a staff) in one hand and a globe in the other. There is another staff behind him, planted in the ground and standing on its own. He looks over the trees, grass, water, and mountains in the distance with a sense of longing. The fact that he holds up one staff while the other is planted signifies the fact that his initial success has only stirred up more ambition within him; he is ready to move on to the next venture. The walls of the balcony symbolizes security, stability, and comfort; he gazes beyond them, showing that he is beginning to wonder if these things are holding him back, rather than simply protecting him. Is it time to take a risk?

The globe in his hand references the phrase: "The world is your oyster." Everything he needs is at his disposal; he needs only to grasp the right tools, and take a bold step forward.

Three of Wands

Upright - Expansion; travel; progress; forward momentum; stepping out of your comfort zone.

Reversed - Getting too comfortable as a big fish in a small pond; stagnation; failed plans; travel problems.

Symbolism - A man stands on the edge of a cliff, with his back turned towards us, looking out over the sea and distant mountains. He wears a similar outfit to that of the Magician in the Major Arcana. He stands by three planted staves, which represent past successes; with his hand on one, he sets his sights on the next leg of his journey. A few ships are sailing in the distance. He might be waiting for a shipment to come in, or he may be ready to board one and sail away.

Four of Wands

Upright - Celebration of hard-earned rewards; relaxation; stability; harmony; joy and relief.

Reversed - Still positive, but muted joy; tainted happiness; something puts a damper on your celebration.

Symbolism - We see a party, but from a distance; in the foreground of the card, four tall Wands are planted and floral garlands are strung up between them, creating a canopy. This denotes victory--a battle hard-fought and well-won! Women with floral wreaths dance behind it, holding bouquets of flowers overhead; behind them stands a castle, a symbol of security and authority.

Five of Wands

Upright - Competition; creative tension; disagreement; a test or rite of passage; sportsmanship, sparring, performative debates or physical fighting.

Reversed - Battling inner demons; healthy competition turning vicious; passive aggression; conflict avoidance; breaking rules for a chance at victory.

Symbolism - Five male figures stand and fight with their Wands as though they are Swords. Some of them are smiling, though, and none of the Wands are pointed directly at any of them. This is a play fight, one in which some of the players have yet to get the hang of how to use a pretend-sword--one character holds it over his shoulder like a baseball bat, while another thrusts his Wand straight up into the air. This represents a competition as a learning experience.

Six of Wands

Upright - Triumph; public recognition; optimism; confidence; victory within reach.

Reversed - Humiliation; betrayed expectations of success; a fall from grace; a failed endeavor; a leader in decline; private recognition; a personal victory unnoticed by others.

Symbolism - A male rides on the back of a white horse with a yellow cloak through a cheering crowd. The man wears a red cape. The color of the horse symbolizes purity of intention; the yellow cloak represents optimism; the red cape denotes boldness and passion. He wears a floral wreath, and carries another wreath on the end of the Wand he bears in his hand--this means a major victory.

Seven of Wands

Upright - Overcoming obstacles on your own; perseverance; personal fortitude and resolve; fighting for what is right; standing alone against many enemies or challenges.

Reversed - Weakness and exhaustion; losing resolve; cowardice; defeat.

Symbolism - A figure stands on the edge of a cliff, with his back to the ledge. Six of the Wands in the card are pointed at him in a threatening manner; he grips the seventh with both hands, not as a Sword, but as a shield across his torso. He wears a shoe on one foot, and boot on another, which may reference indecisiveness, but also may point to the usefulness of distraction tactics, or the strength of character needed to stand apart from the crowd and break the mold.

Eight of Wands

Upright - Swift action; progress achieved at an extraordinary pace; endeavors nearing conclusion; rapid change; air travel.

Reversed - Delays and detours; a lack of progress; deep frustrations; resisting change.

Symbolism - This is one of the few cards in the Tarot deck without a single human character in the illustration. Eight wands soar through the air, soon to land on the ground. Their proximity to earth represents culmination or manifestation; what was once airborne and immaterial will soon become a physical reality.

Nine of Wands

Upright - Tested faith; goals just out of reach; last-minute curveballs or setbacks; resilience and persistence;

Reversed - Giving up; dejection; losing faith; defensive attitude; a person pushed beyond their limits; broken or unacknowledged boundaries.

Symbolism - A figure stands before eight of the nine wands, peering over his shoulder at the others while he holds the ninth in his hands, leaning on it. He wears a bandage on his head and appears exhausted. The bandage represents a wound to the head or ego. He's come so close and yet he still might not make it; he's in danger of becoming too dejected to complete this project, despite all the time and energy already invested in it.

Ten of Wands

Upright - Hard work; carrying the weight of the world; extreme burdens; one final push to complete a major project.

Reversed - Relief; delegation; collapse under pressure; completion; release; responsibilities given up.

Symbolism - A man carries a bundle of ten Wands in his arms, plowing forwards towards a house in the distance. He is building something, and it's nearly complete--but is his enthusiasm to finish leading him to bite off more than he can chew? He looks down at his feet and the Wands block his view of the house in the distance; he is so focused on forward momentum that he can't see how long this journey is, and that he might not make it if he can't find someone to help him carry this load.

Page of Wands

Upright - The Page of Wands is passionate, creative, enthusiastic and charismatic. He is also impulsive--a thrill-seeker who isn't frightened by risk or danger. He is full of new, innovative ideas, and loves the pursuit of discovery. He's a free spirit who won't be tied down or caged in; always moving onward and upward!

Reversed - Immaturity combined with boldness and a love of risk can be a dangerous mix. The reversed Page of Wands is rebellious and impetuous. He wants to unleash his creative energy to the world, and blames others for standing in the way of his potential; what he fails to realize is that he is the one standing in his own way, preventing his own emotional growth.

Symbolism - The Page stands alone with his Wand as a walking staff, glancing up towards the sky, implying lofty ambitions and a daydreamer's attitude. He wears a feather in his cap, which is usually a sign of accomplishment or victory in battle-- but considering his inexperienced rank and lack of correlation to warfare, perhaps this feather is a sign that he has a bit of a chip on his shoulder, or has an overinflated sense of personal capability.

Knight of Wands

Upright - The Knight rides a galloping horse, engaged in a relentless pursuit. He's got his eye on the prize, and enough bravado and confidence to convince obstacles to leap out of his way. He implies an adventure, a chance taken, or a goal pursued without hesitation. He also represents impulsiveness.

Reversed - Step on the breaks; your head and heart are ready to tackle this challenge, but you may have forgotten your physical or material limitations. This card implies that inexperience or lack of planning and preparation can lead to a failed mission. It can also suggest a hot temper, recklessness, or destructive impulsivity.

Symbolism - The Knight rides full steam ahead on an auburn horse. He wears bright red feathers in his helmet, which signifies the passion that drives him forward.

Queen of Wands

Upright - The Queen of Wands comfortable upon her throne. She is satisfied with her lot in life and confident in her abilities. She is independent, but diplomatic and well-liked by others. Finally, she is quite comfortable in her skin.

Reversed - When this card appears upside down, it often references self-serving behaviors. These could be mild and harmless, like introversion or harnessing self-respect, but these behaviors could also be taken to an extreme and serve to create conflict. This card represents the attitude of wanting to have your cake and eat it, too, even if the rest of the world is starving. Think Marie Antoinette.

Symbolism - The Queen sits on a throne holding a wand and a sunflower, symbols of creative power and optimism. The throne is decorated with lion statues, which stands for regality and courage; the throne's back has an ornate pattern and extends up beyond the edge of the card, representing sky-high aspirations and limitless potential. She sits with her knees played open, emitting a calm but inviting sexual energy. If you wish to accept her invitation, though, tread carefully; her black cat sits before her, guarding her with a sneer and a warning hiss.

King of Wands

Upright - This character represents the kind of ruler who can affect positive, lasting change. He is a visionary, a builder, a gifted and moving speaker, and a charismatic leader. Beneath all of that, he is also honest, kind, and genuine. Like Arthur in medieval legend, this man was born to rule.

Reversed - Ruling is tough work; this reversed card can imply impatience with the level of responsibility a leader has been carrying for a long time, or the developed habit of taking shortcuts, cutting corners, or even treating other people as though they are disposable. Perhaps a once honorable leader has grown into a despot or dictator.

Symbolism - The King sits upon a similar throne to that held by the Queen of Wands, decorated with a lion motif. He also wears a lion pendant around his neck. Courage, power, and majesty are clearly very important to him. On the ground by his feet is a salamander, an alchemical symbol of transformation. The King of Wands wants to change the world for the better--or, if he cannot do that, he will at least leave a lasting mark upon it.

CHAPTER 8
The Suit Of Swords

In Tarot, the Suit of Swords concerns matters of the mind. It represents the fine line between intellect used for good and mental power used to promote evil. It also deals with conflict, discord, and hardship.

When we are happy, we feel it emotionally. When our passions are awakened, we often experience the sensation in our muscles. When we are secure, safe, and steadily rooted, we often feel this in our bones and in our stomachs. But we don't often think about these sensations. Strangely enough, though we place a high value on intellect and mental ability, many of us primarily use our minds to solve problems, so the act of thinking isn't generally a pleasant experience. Things that are easy or simple, we do on autopilot and mentally check out, or daydream. When things are enjoyable, we often act without thinking. We only have to use our heads when something goes wrong and must be fixed, or figured out.

The Swords suit doesn't reference the part of your mind that holds pleasant memories, brilliant inventions, or intricate, beautiful dreams for the future. This suit is about the part of your mind that ruminates and nitpicks; the part that can be ruthless, judgmental, or easily angered; the part that grows anxious, but struggles to manifest change; the part that, if left unbalanced by the energies of Cups and Wands, could turn you into your own worst enemy... or someone else's.

This suit isn't all bad. Intellect can be a wonderful thing: a tool for problem-solving, a weapon to outsmart an opponent or cut through illusion and deception in search of truth. But intellect is also, if you'll pardon the pun, a double-edged sword; if it is encouraged without balance by emotion and manifestation, it can easily become a destructive force.

The Suit of Swords also represents power, authority, and force. Power is a two-faced concept--it's something that we sometimes respect and admire, but also something we often resent, envy, and fear.

This suit may be more difficult to interpret through combining number and suit meanings than Cups, Wands, or Pentacles, so guided study of the individual Sword cards is a worthwhile endeavor. The cards can often have positive connotations that reference strife or anguish in the past; for example, the Six of Swords is an optimistic card, pointing to improved conditions ahead, but pointedly acknowledging that this improvement is a long overdue respite from recent conflict and anguish.

The Suit of Swords is connected to the element air. Air, like intellect, is invisible, intangible, unpredictable and volatile. It can be gentle and warm, or sharp, cold, and fierce. Air denotes clarity, truth, and justice. The winds of change will uproot whatever lacks a sturdy foundation or deep roots, tear down the veils that cover secrets and hidden truths, and spread the seed of knowledge and truth throughout the world.

Both Swords and Wands in the Tarot deck are representative of masculine energy; it is perhaps no great coincidence that both items are phallic in shape, and correlate to active, volatile, assertive elements--namely, air and fire.

When a spread is dominated by Sword cards, proceed with caution! This might indicate that the querent's life is already in turmoil of some kind, but if not, it can be a warning that most or all of the querent's options for next steps will lead to some form of conflict or confrontation. Conflict isn't always a bad thing; it can achieve positive ends, clear the air, make way for improvements--but it is awfully unpleasant to face head-on, if only for a short while. That concept summarizes the energy of the Sword cards: they reference difficulties we endure and the walls we push through in order to reach something better.

Ace of Swords

Upright - A message of truth; an epiphany; a mental breakthrough; important knowledge uncovered.

Reversed - Cognitive dissonance; clouded judgment; mental anguish; dishonesty; secrecy.

Symbolism - A hand reaches out of the clouds to offer a Sword with a crown and a torn laurel wreath atop it. The sword has pierced the crown and wreath, a symbol that intellect and mental fortitude can overpower authority and triumph. The Sword is surrounded by gold sparks of flame, symbolizing divine inspiration.

Two of Swords

Upright - Stuck at a crossroads; denial; impassivity; stagnation; indecisiveness; patience; rejecting all available options; closed-mindedness.

Reversed - Forced to make a choice; pushed forward by an external force, despite unwillingness to be moved; a rude awakening; a harsh reality check.

Symbolism - A woman sits blindfolded on a bench with her back to the sea. She holds two Swords in hand and crosses her arms over her chest in the shape of an X. She is at a crossroads, but she refuses to remove the blindfold and make a choice. She would prefer to sit and wait, protected by her blades, for a better option. Above her, the moon hangs in the sky, a symbol that change will come whether it is wanted or not.

Three of Swords

Upright - Heartbreak; love lost; conflict; emotional anguish; the end of an important relationship.

Reversed - Healing; renewed faith in love; ignoring or denying emotional pain; forgiveness; hope for the future.

Symbolism - This iconic illustration is fairly self-explanatory, in terms of symbolic imagery. A heart hangs in the sky below storm clouds, in the rain. It is pierced through by three swords. The heart is being ripped apart. The rain is representative of tears and sorrow.

Four of Swords

Upright - Recuperation and recovery; taking a time out; involuntary rest; a retreat; meditation; self-reflection.

Reversed - Returning to work; exertion and exhaustion; chaos; failure to self-reflect.

Symbolism - A man is laid to rest inside what appears to be a church; a stained-glass window hangs above him, symbolizing the divine light that can only reach him in this state. Three swords hang above him, while one lays horizontal at his side, embedded in the side of his coffin. This symbolizes the need to retreat and reflect upon the defeat that landed him here.

Five of Swords

Upright - A cruelly won victory; success at any cost; conflict; violence; defeat; a lopsided battle.

Reversed - Recovery; healing; reconciliation; restored justice.

Symbolism - A man stands in the foreground of the illustration with three Swords in his hands and two abandoned on the ground by his feet. He looks over his shoulder, leering at two weeping figures--presumably, the men who dropped the two fallen Swords. They turn their backs to us, signaling their humiliation. Overhead, a recent storm is clearing up. The battle is over, but at what cost? The victor does not seem terribly likable, and his triumph may have only come from his unfair advantage.

Six of Swords

Upright - Making the best of a bad situation; a difficult transition; grinning and bearing it; moving forward in spite of emotional anguish. This card can also reference travel by sea.

Reversed - Lack of movement; obsessive rumination; stuck in the past; unable to move on; heels dug in the sand; refusal to accept change; stuck in a vicious cycle or rut. This reversed card embodies the spirit of someone who will not abandon a sinking ship.

Symbolism - A male figure stands, navigating a rowboat, while a woman and child sit in front of him in the boat. Six swords are protruding from the vessel, hilts facing up. This may suggest that the boat itself is damaged, and could start to sink at any moment-- still, the man rows on. What else can he do?

Seven of Swords

Upright - Cunning; secret betrayal; criminal activity; getting away with bad behavior; using intellect to skirt consequences; strategizing.

Reversed - Caught in the act; attempting to make amends; betrayal of the self; risks taken without forethought.

Symbolism - A man tiptoes through a military camp, arms filled with bundles of Swords, grinning. He might be sneaking in to attack, but since he's turned his back to the tents, he's more likely stealing. He looks quite pleased with himself, proud of his deceit.

Eight of Swords

Upright - Standing in your own way; caged in by negative thoughts; victim mentality; bondage and imprisonment.

Reversed - Freedom; releasing negativity; escape; attitude adjustment; self-empowerment.

Symbolism - A woman stands, bound and blindfolded, on a seashore with eight swords plunged into the stand, surrounding her. Everything about this scene symbolizes restriction, or the inability to move. But there's no one else around, and she seems resigned to her fate; is it possible she put herself in this position?

Nine of Swords

Upright - Rumination; anxiety; insomnia; restlessness; fear; night terrors.

Reversed - Emotional weight lifted off your shoulders; unwarranted optimism; denial.

Symbolism - A woman sits upright in bed, burying her face in her hands, clearly distressed. Nine swords hover above her bed, all horizontal. She has conflict in her mind, and it is preventing her from sleeping.

Ten of Swords

Upright - A devastating loss; betrayal; failure despite best efforts to succeed; painful defeat; grief; the sense that all is lost.

Reversed - Climbing back up from rock bottom; a fresh start; recovery.

Symbolism - This card's illustration is fairly easy to read. A figure lies face down in the dirt with ten swords plunged into his back. He doesn't bleed, though, which tells us this card isn't about physical death or violence--it's about mental pain. In the background, the sun is just beginning to crest the horizon; brighter days lie ahead.

Page of Swords

Upright - He may be young and inexperienced, but this Page is ready for a fight, and you probably wouldn't want to cross him. He is independent but defensive; curious, and sharp as a tack. He values knowledge and is eager to learn, but also carries his own innovative spark, full of original ideas. He is ready to defend these ideas against attack or theft at the drop of a hat.

Reversed - This reversed card symbolizes the act of getting in over your head, or walking unprepared into a battle of wits against someone has planned ahead for this fight. Furthermore, it can represent immaturity of thought, lack of manifestation, poor communication, and impulsive action. Imagine a child who thinks himself smarter than any adult he knows but lacks the emotional maturity or philosophical awareness to recognize his own shortcomings.

Symbolism - The Page stands with his sword raised, ready to swing--but where is his opponent? All that surrounds him are clouds, which are beginning to dissipate; they may represent the lifting of a mental fog.

Knight of Swords

Upright - Someone needs a hero, and the Knight of Swords is ready and eager to fill that role. He loves a good fight in the name of justice, and he's bold enough to face his opponents head-on. This Knight is assertive, cuts to the chase, and doesn't waste time.

Reversed - When this card is upturned, it can reference a person who talks a lot about standing up for what is right but cowers in fear, or hides, when push comes to shove. It may also describe someone whose alleged quest for justice is merely a disguised thirst for violence and domination. Finally, it can describe a warrior who starts the journey strong but loses steam before the battle is won.

Symbolism - The Knight rides, full steam ahead, under a stormy sky, sword drawn and raised. The storm represents conflict. There are birds drawn on the horse's reigns and the Knight's cape, symbolizing speed and reminding us of the Knight's elemental energy, which is air.

Queen of Swords

Upright - The Queen of Swords is cool-tempered and level-headed. She thinks before she speaks and never parts her lips impulsively. She is rational, calm, and thoughtful.

Reversed - Rationality is replaced with callous behavior and cruelty. Her calm demeanor has become pessimistic and bitter. In her pursuit of truth and justice, she has forgotten to value humanity and is now willing to manipulate, betray, or berate others in order to achieve her goals.

Symbolism - The Queen sits on her throne with a sword raised in one hand; her other hand is lifted as if in blessing, or to make a proclamation, but her lips remain sealed and straight as an arrow. Her stance reflects that of Lady Justice, but she holds no scales. Her raised Sword shows us she values truth above all else. Despite her austere face, her throne is adorned with butterflies and chubby-cheeked cherubs: symbols of softness and femininity. Her character is a balance of masculine and feminine energy, the soft and the hard, the assertive and the passive.

King of Swords

Upright - This is a leader who rarely smiles, but not necessarily because he is unkind or cold-hearted. He is stern but fair; smart, but not full of himself; authoritative, but not power-hungry. The King of Swords has reached the throne by using his intellect and derives personal satisfaction from performing his duties well.

Reversed - The reversed King of Swords points to corrupted power. This character believes he alone is above the law and will do whatever he feels is necessary to secure more and more power. But he will do so quietly, and use his intellect to avoid being seen. He may also lash out at those in his inner circle, but to the public, he will present a calm, though austere, face.

Symbolism - The King of Swords sits upon his throne with Sword in hand. His throne is adorned with butterflies, just like the Queen of this suit, and it's back extends beyond the card's frame; this symbolizes limitless communion with the divine, as well as the transformative power of thought. His robes are high necked and conceal every part of his body except for the face and hands; this symbolizes a connection to religious or spiritual authority, mirroring the apparel of the clergy in the Christian church. These garments also point to his inability to be emotionally vulnerable.

CHAPTER 9
The Suit Of Pentacles

The Suit of Pentacles was once more commonly known as the Suit of Coins; therefore, this suit's association with matters of finance, business, and work is fairly easy to recognize. Pentacles are about more than just money, though; they are connected to the element of earth and reference the physical, material, and external concerns of the human consciousness. That includes health and physical fitness; shelter, safety, and security; wealth, in both financial and immaterial forms (such as success, recognition, accolades, social affluence, and so on); strength, beauty, and prowess.

This suit is strongly correlated to the ego. It often references the querent's self-esteem or self-image.

While the illustrations of some Pentacles cards appear to depict abundance, wealth, joy and celebration, there are also plenty in this suit that focus on the hard work needed to achieve such ends.

Ace of Pentacles

Upright - A new job or career; an investment opportunity; a promotion; an offering.

Reversed - Opportunities that never pan out; bad investments; inability to find work.

Symbolism - A hand reaches out of the clouds to offer a Pentacle or Coin. Below it is a beautiful garden of white lilies and green vines, with an arched gateway leading to the mountains in the distance. This hints at the promise of a new opportunity.

Two of Pentacles

Upright - Work-life balance; managing multiple things at once; time management; keeping busy; making ends meet.

Reversed - Inability to manage time; an overwhelming to-do list; dropped priorities and failure to honor promises.

Symbolism - A juggler dances in a clown's costume. He juggles two pentacles encapsulated by the infinity loop, which represents limitless potential, as well as the fact that his work never ends. Behind him, ships are sailing on a choppy sea, a symbol of volatility, imbalance, and risk.

Three of Pentacles

Upright - Teamwork and creative collaboration; talent and skill coming together; apprenticeship; growth; new possibilities; potential.

Reversed - Poor teamwork; inattention to detail; cut corners and shortcuts; disharmony; insisting on taking all the credit for a team effort.

Symbolism - Three figures stand within a chapel; two seem to be advising the third on an installation of some kind. It seems clear that all three figures value the opinions of others. The youngest and lowest ranked character stands on a bench to reach the installation, representing the strength that can come from combining the strength and agility of youth with the wisdom of experience.

Four of Pentacles

Upright - Financial stability; conservative spending habits; saving over spending.

Reversed - Wealth hoarding; unreasonable anxiety; time to let loose, if only just a little.

Symbolism - A crowned man sits before a city landscape. A Pentacle rests upon his crown, but he also stamps two others down under his boots, and grips one tightly in his hands. For someone with so much wealth, why is he grasping these Pentacles so tightly? He almost appears worried they'll float away like balloons if he loosens his grip. He's turned his back to the city, where he could put these coins to good use.

Five of Pentacles

Upright - Falling on tough times; financial powerlessness; poverty; scarcity mindset; stress and fear.

Reversed - Renewed hope; recovery; accepting help; finding a new pathway forward. When you hit bottom, the only direction you can go is up.

Symbolism - Two impoverished figures struggle to move forward through a wintry haze. One is on crutches, and wears a bell around his neck to warn others of his approach; this is a historical reference to leprosy, which reminds us that the poor don't only struggle with poverty, but with discrimination as well. They walk before a stained-glass window of Pentacles, most likely a church; this shows that their only hope is spiritual salvation.

Six of Pentacles

Upright - Spreading the wealth; giving and receiving abundance; charity work; mercy; compassion; benevolence.

Reversed - Greed; stinginess; inability to ask for help; unpaid debts; financial injustice.

Symbolism - A benevolent figure stands before two kneeling ones. The standing man holds a scale, symbolizing fairness and an egalitarian outlook, while he drops coins into the hands of one of the kneeling men. He smiles as he does so, and the two kneeling men smile back up at him. When we share our wealth, everyone benefits.

Seven of Pentacles

Upright - Preparing to dive back into work; perseverance; planning ahead; reflecting on past accomplishments.

Reversed - An inability to work or earn money; lack of personal application or initiative; impatience with the task at hand.

Symbolism - A lone figure stands beside a bush that appears to be growing pentacles. It's time to harvest them, but at this point, the figure is still deciding how best to tackle the project.

Eight of Pentacles

Upright - Progress; being in the zone; hard work; developing mastery.

Reversed - Loss of interest in the task at hand; problematic perfectionism; misdirected energy; slow work.

Symbolism - A young man sits at a workbench, hammering at a Pentacle, head bent low in focus. There is a pleasant landscape behind him, yet he sees nothing but the work at hand.

Nine of Pentacles

Upright - Earned rewards; personal wealth; self-care; luxury; relaxing isolation.

Reversed - Discontent; jealousy; overworking; a sense of never being satisfied with what one has.

Symbolism - A woman stands alone in a lush garden full of grape vines and flowers. She appears content with her solitude. A hooded falcon is perched on her hand, representing discipline. On the ground before her, a snail creeps along, reminding us that haste is unnecessary in this context.

Ten of Pentacles

Upright - A windfall or jackpot; overwhelming success; a lasting sense of security.

Reversed - The divisive power of wealth; greed; failure to invest wisely; money or resources squandered.

Symbolism - Three generations of a family are gathered in a courtyard below an archway, which symbolizes the crossing of a border or ascension to a new echelon. The father in the scene holds a Wand, perhaps implying that they have reached this place through his invention and entrepreneurial skills.

Page of Pentacles

Upright - Pages are often viewed as messengers; this Page brings news of good fortune, financial success, and new opportunities. He is young, ambitious, determined, focused, and achievement oriented. He also has a sense of optimism in regards to attaining wealth and accolades. This is the type of young person who could convince you to invest in their new business, despite their lack of experience; his charisma and obvious faith in his own abilities make all the difference.

Reversed - This can represent a money-making venture that has left you in debt when you expected to be rolling in dough. It's not just pure bad luck, though; this references a bad experience that should be learned from. Perhaps with increased focus, better planning, or more realistic goals, success could have been reached. For now, though, you must recognize that the current plan is financially impractical, and needs to be altered or thrown out entirely.

Symbolism - The Page stands in a lush meadow on a bed of flowers; behind him, there are trees and mountains in the distance. But his gaze is fixed on the orbed pentacle floating above his hands. He looks at it like he is in love, and can hardly see anything else. The world is open to him, full of possibilities--but his financial goal is all he cares about.

Knight of Pentacles

Upright - The Knight of Pentacles is active and honorable, but not necessarily eager to fight. He represents a sense of duty, diligence, and level-headed rationality. He is pragmatic and responsible. He knows that much of his strength comes from knowing when to take action, and when to simply wait.

Reversed - This reversed card references a character who has lost their focus and cannot seem to get their head on straight. The problem is most likely a lack of self-discipline or distractibility.

Symbolism - The Knight rides a black horse, standing still as he looks over an open meadow with a recently plowed field. He holds a Pentacle in hand and looks over the meadow with satisfaction, appreciating the value of a job well done.

Queen of Pentacles

Upright - The Queen of Pentacles is materially wealthy, but not necessarily concerned with frivolity or greed. She earns well because she feels a sense of responsibility to those who rely on her. Her primary concern is maintaining a safe, secure, and sturdy home for herself and her loved ones. She is maternal, protective, practical and generous; the ultimate earth mother. She is able to enjoy the fruits of her labor, too, so long as all her loved ones are taken care of first.

Reversed - Here, the Queen's urge to protect her family has spiraled out of control. She has lost trust in outsiders and now feels the impulse to hoard her wealth and board up the windows. She has developed a mentality of scarcity where none actually exists. Or, alternatively, she may have grown tired of spending her money on others, and become exclusively self-serving.

Symbolism - The Queen sits upon a colorful throne in a lush garden grove, gazing down at the Pentacle in her hand with gratitude and serenity. A rabbit hops through the grove, a symbol of fertility. Since she holds the rounded pentacle near her womb, creating the shape of a pregnant belly, some may see this card as a reference to family planning.

King of Pentacles

Upright - The King of Pentacles is all about amassing wealth--but, like the Queen of this suit, his actions aren't necessarily motivated by greed. He is a leader who uses wealth to provide for his family and his people. The money is used to protect them, to keep them warm and dry and fed. He has enough wealth that he can afford to be benevolent. You might think of him as a Wall Street tycoon, business owner, or industry mogul.

Reversed - The reversed King of Pentacle has been corrupted by greed. Despite his wealth, he is stingy and ungenerous; he is only willing to spend money on that which benefits him personally. Alternatively, he may indeed be a financial failure who still insists on living like a King, racking up debt and leeching off of those around him.

Symbolism - The King sits upon a throne surrounded by evidence of his wealth: flowers, fruit, and growing vines. His castle towers in the background. He holds a Pentacle and a scepter and wears a wreath of flowers above his crown, as well as a floral motif on his robes. The throne is decorated with ram's heads, a reference to the Taurus sign and earth element.

CHAPTER 10
Starting Simple

Now that we've begun to build a personal connection to the cards and developed some understanding of their symbolism, it's time to dive in and start practicing! You may be lucky enough to have a partner, friend, or group of fellow cartomancers to practice with, trading readings and drawing from each other's perspectives; still, if you are the only Tarot enthusiast in your circle, there's no reason why you can't practice on your own. Cartomancy healers can absolutely read their own spreads; this is how some spiritual and metaphysical healers use the Tarot deck as a living, ever-changing holy book, looking to the cards for personalized guidance from the divine. Even in this case, though, it is best to acknowledge your own limitations and weaknesses before performing a self-directed reading, and always bounce any radical or extreme ideas divined from the cards off of a third party before executing plans or taking drastic steps.

Preparing for a reading

Whether you plan to read for yourself or to sit for a fellow cartomancer, it's always a good idea to prepare yourself physically, mentally, and emotionally beforehand. If you sit down for a reading distracted, unfocused, or uncertain of what you want to get from it, you're likely to get a spread of cards that reflects this state, and divine nothing from them but confusion and mixed messages.

A good first step is meditation or any other practice that helps you to relax and clear your mind, like a bath, or a solo hike in nature. The goal is to get deeply in touch with your feelings and emotions, which are not to be mistaken for thoughts. Have you been overwhelmed lately? Uninspired? Hypersensitive? Emotionally numb? Happy, melancholy, bored, or furious? If you don't know what you're feeling, you won't understand how your emotions influence your interpretation of the cards.

You will also want to reconnect with your innermost desires, which should not be confused for necessities. Regardless of what you can afford, what you have time for, or what is accessible--what do you really want at this point in time? What preoccupies your thoughts while you wait in line at the bank, or finish household chores? It can be easy to fall into the habit of framing this question in material terms, but try to think bigger. If you were a magician, what changes could you make in your life that might give you lasting happiness, rather than a momentary thrill? A brand-new luxury car is an easy item to fantasize about, but the vehicle itself may simply represent a deeper desire for ease and convenience of travel, combined with a visible status symbol. Perhaps the desire for a new car truly represents a desire for power and recognition.

By re-centering yourself and checking in with your emotional body, you should have an easier time discerning exactly what it is you hope to get out of your reading. Are you in the right frame of mind for tough love, or to receive advice that will be difficult to implement? How will you react if the cards deliver a disappointing message? Alternatively, are you feeling open to new possibilities? Are you feeling cynical, and skeptical of cards that might point to good fortune or victory in the near future? Are you hoping the cards will reinforce a decision you've already made internally but have yet to manifest? Or, instead, are you hoping the cards will talk you out of a relationship or behavior that you know in your gut, is no longer serving you? Are you willing to let the cards surprise you with the guidance they provide?

Once you've developed some awareness of your current emotional state, it's a good idea to check in with your reader, especially if you don't know them very well at the start of the reading. There's no reason to expect a cartomancer to be clairvoyant unless they specifically market themselves as such. What a Tarot reader offers is insight, understanding, and guidance; they are not mind-readers, so if there's anything you feel they should know before beginning your reading, it's up to you to communicate it. Tell your reader about your emotions, physical feelings, concerns, and apprehensions before posing your question. The more information you provide, the more accurate and insightful you can expect your reading to be.

Selecting a question

You can expect a far more rewarding and satisfying reading if you make a point of selecting your questions ahead of time, and choosing them wisely.

If you know you'll be working with a novice cartomancer (even if that novice is yourself), it's smart to choose a prompt that takes a bit of pressure off of the reader. Steer clear of questions about life-or-death matters, or prompts that ask for advice on dire financial matters or health problems. It may be tempting to choose a question with yes-or-no answer, but in actuality, these kinds of questions can be too limiting and specific for a reader who is fairly new to the Tarot deck. Instead, aim to construct an open-ended question; queries that begin with the words "how," "what," or "why" will generally lead you in the right direction, rather than questions that begin with words like "when," "where," or "will."

For instance: "When will I get over this heartbreak?" is a tough question to pose to the cards, especially since their meanings have almost no correlation to days, weeks, months, or years--only seasons. Instead, you might ask: "What can I do to mend my broken heart?" or "How can I know when I'm ready to invite new love into my life?"

Another great way to formulate questions for novice readers is to ask after a general impression of an experience. For example: "I'm starting a new job next month; how will my transition into this new position go?" Or, alternatively: "I'm aiming to refocus and apply myself in school this year; what can I do to make the most of this semester?"

This is a good formula for questions posed to a more experienced Tarot reader, too, though you can feel free to pose more complex, serious, and important prompts with them. You can dive into deeper matters--ask for advice on health concerns, financial matters, marriage and divorce, family planning, and so on. It may be tempting to ask the cards if you will achieve your dreams, how you can become a billionaire, where you'll meet your soulmate, or when you might ultimately pass away, but remember: even expert

Tarot readers cannot provide reliably accurate answers to these questions, primarily because they aren't what the cards are designed for.

It's a good idea to keep your prompts focused on the self; asking questions about other people's lives will ultimately leave you, the cartomancer, and the cards themselves, confused and uncertain, because none of you will have as much information as is necessary to gain insight on these matters. Furthermore, the cards are meant to give you guidance on how to move forward; the universe will not urge you to step forward to fight somebody else's battles, only your own. You can't be given advice on how to manage situations that are beyond your control. Use prompts to show the universe that you're ready to take ownership of your life and responsibility for your own future. For example: "How can I foster trust in my relationship?" is a far better question than: "Is my partner going to cheat on me?" or "How can I make sure my lover doesn't fall for someone else?"

Do your best to broaden the focus of your prompts. The more specific your questions are, the more information and guidance you are shutting out. As an illustrative example: if you, as the querent, are handling some difficulties in your marriage in regards to family planning, it would be understandably tempting to ask the cards: "How can we resolve this dispute?" Or: "Why can't we agree on whether we want to have children or not?" Or even: "What can I do to convince my partner we are ready to have a family?"

In truth, though, you might find more useful guidance if you are able to broaden the scope of these questions beyond the current predicament. You might ask: "How will our marriage progress?" Or: "What will this relationship bring to me?"

The difference is that this second set of questions allows the possibility of a surprising, unexpected answer. Perhaps your plan to have a child will be altered by unforeseen circumstances-- infertility or other health concerns, or a career move. The universe may have plans to deliver you a child that isn't biologically yours-- a sudden opportunity to adopt a child that is in need, or already near and dear to your heart, might present itself. The first set of questions doesn't allow the cards to hint at these possibilities, but the second set gives both the deck and the reader some more flexibility.

Imagine your card reading as a journey. If you choose questions that force the reader to stick to a predetermined route, they'll spend the whole trip with their nose buried in the map and fail to notice all the beauty around them or the intriguing side-roads that aren't marked on the map at all. A better alternative is to set your sights on a direction or destination, and then allow yourself to wander freely. You may get lost along the way, and never reach the predetermined destination--but if you stick to the map exclusively, how can you ever know if that destination is the best place for you to end up?

Focussing your prompts on the present can be helpful. You cannot change the past, and Tarot is not hypnotism--it can't be relied upon to unearth repressed memories or expose old secrets. You might turn to Tarot in hopes that you'll find a roadmap for your future-- but what if your fate is not yet set in stone? What if the choices you make today could impact or alter your future trajectory? What would be the point of mapping the future of your current career, when tomorrow, you might have a life-changing experience that pushes you to go back to school and pursue work in an entirely different field? Instead, ask the Tarot deck to illuminate just the next few steps of your journey, rather than predicting its endpoint or tracing back to its origin.

Finally, it's a good idea to dream up a few follow-up questions, or alternate lines of questioning, just in case the first prompt turns up an answer that is short and simple, disappointing, or just plain confusing. Tarot readers are merely human, and some are better suited to certain subject matters than others. If you're working with a professional cartomancer, you may find, upon first meeting them, that you don't really click, or that their response to your initial question feels incomplete, off the mark, or unearths a disparity in your value systems. As a simple example: your cartomancer might presume that you hope one day to get married and have children, and allow this assumption about your values to affect their divination technique, not realizing that you dislike children and harbor little faith in monogamy. Even in a situation like this, try not to let yourself get discouraged or to become dismissive of the reader's abilities; instead, let them know that you feel you might not be on the same page, clarify your feelings about the previous spread, and ask to try a different line of questioning. Be kind, but be honest, too. Chances are, your cartomancer will appreciate your candor.

Now that you are relaxed, centered, and prepared with a question (or a few!), it's time to close your eyes, take a deep breath, and dive into your reading.

One card reading

An excellent place for beginners to start is with a one card spread. Why? Because it uses one single card from the deck--that's it. In this spread, the reader doesn't need to factor in the context of other cards, weigh Major and Minor Arcana cards differently, look for outliers or decipher the meanings of upright and reversed cards. There's just one card, and it's either upright or reversed; the rest is up to you.

Ready? Let's get started!

First, set up a space for your reading. This doesn't need to be anything fancy or costly; you could even choose to do your readings outdoors, in nature, on a boulder or tree stump, so long as the cards don't blow away in the wind. If you do choose to stay indoors, though, aim to create a space that promotes focus, calm, and peace of mind. Quiet is best for clarity of thought. Make sure there is adequate light, and a clean, stable surface where you can lay your cards out without worrying about staining, bending, or otherwise damaging them. You may want to elevate this to a sacred space by decorating with crystals, candles, geomancy grids, smudge sticks, or any other relics that inspire you and help you to feel connected to nature and the divine.

Choose a question. If you're practicing to improve your skills, it's a good idea to jot down a list of questions and be prepared to log your results in your Tarot journal.

Once you have a question in mind, close your eyes and meditate on it for a minute or two. What are your hopes? What are your fears? What seems like the most predictable outcome? What result would surprise or shock you?

Open your eyes. Take a deep breath. You can pose the question to the deck silently or aloud, but either way, be sure you do so with purpose. Clear your throat, set up a crystal grid, or light a candle if you get an inkling that the universe isn't listening very attentively.

You'll want to begin shuffling the deck while the question is still fresh in your mind, or has just rolled off your tongue. While shuffling, keep the question playing on repeat in your head like a broken record.

You're done shuffling whenever you feel the instinct to stop. Cut the deck at random, and draw one card for yourself. Place it on a surface with the illustration side down.

Take another deep breath. If your mind has wandered at all while shuffling the cards, this is a chance to re-focus on your question.

Now flip the card over, revealing the illustration.

Take as much time as you need to ponder it. You might stare at the image for five or ten minutes before even attempting to decode its symbolic meaning. Try to listen to your instincts and embrace your visceral reactions to the card before your mind starts working on the suit and number formula, or trying to recall information gathered while studying the Major Arcana cards. Remember there are no wrong answers here. Any strong feelings that this card elicits in you should be taken seriously, even if they seem to be at odds with its commonly accepted interpretation.

After you've done this, you can feel free to consult this book, or any other Tarot guide, for further explanation of the card you've drawn.

Ultimately, it is up to you to decide when you've found a satisfactory answer. You may not find any single guidebook or website that seems to hit the nail right on the head, but instead decide to pick and choose aspects of several different schools of thought, and devise your own interpretation. You should be able to feel it in your gut when you've found an interpretation that addresses your personal needs and circumstances.

If not, try not to worry. The beauty of a one card spread is that it is fairly quick and easy; you can always try again, and again, and again. Eventually, your intuition will begin to resonate with the cards more deeply, and you'll feel stronger reactions to the cards you draw.

Two card reading

The next step is to expand your repertoire, but slowly. Jumping from one card spread to a Romany spread of twenty-one cards is an easy way to overwhelm yourself and ruin your enjoyment of cartomancy as an art form.

Instead, work on a two card spread. For this reading, you can use the same space, surface, and preparation techniques as you did for a one card spread; this time, though, you'll want to choose a question that involves choice or duality. Are you at a fork in the road of your life's journey? Are you struggling to devote yourself to one of two possible career paths? Are you torn between two relationship partners? Are you weighing the pros and cons of settling down close to home, versus moving halfway across the world? Any prompt that asks the cards to compare and contrast two options will be well suited to this spread.

Again, close your eyes, focus on your question, and speak it aloud if you wish. Now shuffle your deck, and cut it. Draw two cards, and lay them face down, side by side. You might choose to refocus on your question right here, briefly, before revealing the cards.

Now turn both over. In this spread, order doesn't particularly matter (though in more complex spreads, it will). Look carefully at the illustrations on each card, and try to decide which one correlates to which option. Aside from their interpretable significance, the card's illustrations tell stories. If you're struggling to see how one (or both) relates to the question at hand, consult this book, or others, to gain further insight into its meaning.

Three card reading

At this point, you may be ready for something a bit more complex.

A three card spread can be interpreted in one of two ways: the cards can represent the sitter's past, present, and future; or, alternatively, they can signify two options, as in a two-card spread, with the third card providing advice, or an extra nudge in one direction or the other.

For the past, present, and future spread follow the steps used for the two card spread but lay out a third card. Arrange them face down from left to right, and aim to reveal and interpret each before upturning the next card. Novices will get the most out of this practice because they can focus on the cards one at a time, without getting confused about how each of them impacts the others or overwhelmed by their interconnectedness.

The first card you flip will represent the past realities that led the querent to ask this question. If you are working with a sitter, this is a good place to evaluate the accuracy of your intuition. Don't be afraid to ask them questions if the card doesn't seem to be giving you much to go on.

The second card you upturn will represent the present day or the current circumstances that led the querent to pose this question. Here, practice relating the cards to each other by trying to find a narrative line to draw from the first card to the second. If they are part of the same suit, this can be fairly easy; however, if they mix suits, involve reversed cards and Major Arcana characters, connections can become more complicated. Take your time considering, and listen to your inner voice. You may need to consider several different possibilities before settling on an interpretation that feels right to you and resonates with the sitter.

The third card pulled will give the querent a glimpse into the future. Tarot cards can rarely predict specific outcomes for the future-- dates, numbers, exact locations, yes or no questions, and so on-- but in this spread, the third card will represent the general feelings or themes that the querent can look forward to in regards to their question. This is based on only one card, but you can also factor in the previous two cards and look for connections. Once all three are upturned, take a moment to clear your mind of your preconceived understanding of the cards, and simply look at the illustrations. In this order, do they tell a story? Do you see color themes echoed in all three cards? Or items that are represented in all three, despite varying suits?

Now, let's walk through another three card spread option. This time, follow the steps for a two-card spread, laying out a third card face down beside them, all in a row from left to right, and upturn the first two cards at the same time. Examine them and determine which card represents which of the querent's options.

Take some time with these two cards before even touching the third. Ask the sitter questions: how do they feel about the colors, lines, and themes illustrated on these cards? Do they find them beautiful? Ugly? Strange? Mystifying? Laughable? The querent's reactions to the cards matter just as much as their commonly agreed upon meanings. Choice is personal; there is no objective right or wrong answer, only a matter of the querent's taste and values.

When you and the sitter have discussed the two option cards thoroughly, go ahead and flip over the advice card. Pay close attention to suits: if the third card is an upright Cup card, it may indicate that the sitter should pick whatever option fulfills their emotional needs, or whichever option their gut instincts tell them to choose; if it is an upright Wand card, it may be urging them to go with the choice that inspires their creativity or allows them to manifest their dreams; if you find a Sword card in this position, it could imply that the sitter should go with the rational, logical choice, or alternatively, that the more difficult choice will bring some hardship, but prove to be worth it after difficulties are overcome; finally, if the third card belongs to the Suit of Pentacles, this may imply that the choice will ultimately be defined by material realities and limitations, such as what the sitter can afford, what their body can handle physically, what their career demands of them, and so on.

Of course, if the third card belongs to the Major Arcana, you shouldn't feel any shame in consulting this book and other guides for insight before you decipher its message.

Again, look for thematic connections. If there is a color that dominates the first and third cards, but not the second, this may imply that the first card option is the most obvious or sensible choice, in line with the querent's values, beliefs, desires, and capabilities. It can be tempting to weigh Major Arcana cards as more important or more powerful than those of the Minor Arcana, and in some spreads, you may want to do so--but any spread with three cards or less requires readers to weigh them equally.

Finally, recognize that the third card may not be steering the sitter towards either option. There may be an elusive third choice, an alternate path forward which the sitter isn't even aware of. If you're really struggling to draw a connection between the third card and either of the first two, consider this possibility, and turn to the third card's classic interpretation for insight into what this alternative option might look like. Again, ask your querent about their lives, and their feelings about the cards pulled (though you may ask that they refrain from touching them). The more you know, the more accurate and useful your intuitive advice can be.

CHAPTER 11
Complex Layouts

Now that you've practiced some rudimentary spreads, you may be ready to move on to some more complex layouts. Read on for step-by-step instructions to lead you through some of the most popular divination spreads. To best prepare for these, ask your sitter for a very open-ended question or prompt--for instance, "I'm going to move next month; how is that going to do?" Or: "I'm feeling stuck and uninspired by my career these days; what should I do now?" The Celtic Cross spread is a notable exception, as it can address specific inquiries quite effectively.

The Horseshoe spread

This spread uses seven cards. Its name may be a bit misleading, as the cards are typically arranged in a V shape rather than a U. Many cartomancers will shuffle and cut the deck while the querent focuses on their question, and allow the querent to blow on the deck or to touch it through a soft barrier (use a cloth, for example, so that they can hold the cards without actually touching them) before they cut it. They will then lay the cards out one at a time, with each subsequent card overlapping the corner of the previous card. The fourth card is the anchor of the shape--the low point of the V.

For this particular spread, it can be helpful to compartmentalize card meanings. The fifth card in this spread will have very little impact on your interpretation of the first two, for example, but may weigh heavily in your understanding of the sixth and seventh cards. Discuss these connections aloud with your sitter as you pull the cards--that way, the connections won't become tangled or muddled in your head.

In order from left to right, the cards correlate to:

1. The past events that have placed the querent in their current position.
2. The current realities of the querent's life that prompted their question.

3. The unseen or unacknowledged influences that inform the querent's feelings (this could reference the phases of the moon, parental influence, the ego, repressed emotions, health issues, or even world events).
4. This card represents the querent and gives both the reader and the sitter insight into how their personality will affect the outcome of this situation.
5. How others view the situation or how they feel about the querent.
6. Advises next steps for the querent.
7. Hints at the most likely outcome or result of actions taken, as advised by the sixth card.

The Pentagram spread

Despite the implications of its name, this layout actually uses six or seven cards, rather than five. It is often used by Wiccans, Pagans, and those who worship the occult.

The first step is to choose a Significator--a card to represent the querent. The reader can choose this card purposefully--no need to shuffle the deck and draw a card at random here. Choose a card, ideally from the Major Arcana, that signifies the querent's current emotional or mental state, or their role in the situation that they're seeking guidance to manage. This may require you to perform a little get-to-know-you interview before the reading begins. Be sure to explain your choice to the sitter as you lay this card down as the center of your pentagram; if you've chosen the Devil, or the Hanged Man, for example, make sure your sitter understands that these cards are not condemnations, and can have positive as well as negative meanings.

After laying out this card, shuffle the deck while meditating on the sitter's question, or discussing it aloud. Then lay out five cards to surround the Significator, each corresponding to a point of a star. You may want to create or purchase a spread board that has the pentagram drawn upon it to guide you, but this isn't necessary. Just make sure one card is directly above the significator; place two cards to the left, one slightly above and one slightly below the center; then mirror this card placement on the right side as well. Lay them out and read them in clockwise order.

The top right card corresponds to the element of earth and represents stability and physical matters. This card points to the querent's present realities, and what grounds them. Does the querent feel boxed in? Chained down or tethered? What is serving to hold them back from manifesting change, or accomplishing their goals? This card also represents the recent past: the circumstances that landed the querent here, the routines they've gotten comfortable with, and so on.

The lower right card is related to the element of air, and concerns thought and communication. This represents the querent's hopes, anxieties, fears, and ideas; it can also correlate to the advice or information the querent is receiving from other people. This card often represents the root of the issue.

The lower left card is linked to the element of fire, which is both a creative and destructive force. This card points to the energies and manifestations that are impacting the situation. What is the querent's will? What have they done (or what might they do moving forward) to accomplish their goals? What is driving them? And finally, how much of this situation is intangible (existing only within the mind), and how much of it grounded in reality?

The upper left card is related to water, the element of intuition, emotion, and the divine feminine. This card represents the querent's inner voice--what their gut is telling them to do. It also points to the near future.

The sixth card can be the first card drawn and the last one read, placed at the star's apex, above the significator. This card is connected to the fifth element of spirit, and represents totality or culmination; it summarizes the message that the previous four cards have laid out as one full concept. This also points to the final outcome, or result.

Alternatively, you might choose to lay out a seventh card with this spread, separate from the Pentagram shape, above its upper right-hand corner. This seventh card will represent the unknown, unseen, and mystical forces that are impacting the situation. This card is removed from the star shape because it generally points to forces that are beyond the querent's control. It can be useful to lay out this final card after placing and reading the previous six, especially if you're struggling to see a unified story or understand the message of the sixth card (the star's apex, and "final" outcome). It can be a real game-changer.

The Romany Spread

The Romany spread is also sometimes called the Gypsy spread; it's one of the oldest traditional divination layouts.

The methodology of this spread is fairly simple, but it uses a whole lot of cards. It's best to set aside a hefty chunk of time to analyze this spread; trying to rush through it will quickly overwhelm, confound, and exhaust you. Prepare yourself for a chatty reading-- you'll want to talk your way through the interpretation process, so as not to lose track of your place in the story the cards are trying to tell you.

This layout is great for sitters who may not have specific questions; perhaps start by simply discussing the querent's current life circumstances and mood; look into anything causing them stress, melancholy, confusion, or anticipation. Also ask the sitter for some insight into what makes them feel happy, safe, and calm. It's also very useful for querents who have multiple interconnected issues, and are struggling to untangle their thoughts or feelings about them.

This spread echoes the three card spread by addressing the past, present, and future; but instead of using three cards, it uses three rows of seven cards each. The center row describes the sitters current circumstances; the top row tells a story about their past; finally, the bottom row explains possibilities for the future. Some card readers may switch the meanings of the top and middle row, but this is the more traditional route.

As a reader, you could then dive deeper into the meanings by analyzing the seven columns in turn; in groups of three, they will create mini-narrative arcs, flashing back to the past that informs the present, gaining insight into the current circumstances, and then proceeding into the future.

The first column will reference physical realities, and social influence--this pertains to friends, family, and lovers, but also money, career, and health.

The second column will speak to the emotional body--the sitter's feelings, wishes, desires, and fears, as well as their intuitive abilities.

The third column concerns the mind--thoughts, ideas, and plans. Also philosophical questions or struggles.

The fourth column is about querent's core identity. Who are they today? Who were they in the past? How will they evolve in the future?

The fifth column hints at the unknown: surprises, unexpected events, curveballs, as well as mysteries, secrets, esoteric knowledge and spiritual energy.

The sixth column predicts the near future or the querent's next few steps.

The seventh column points to the distant future or ultimate outcome.

Alternatively, some readers may use the seven columns to predict the next seven days of the sitter's life, reading each column in order.

The Celtic Cross spread

While this spread uses fewer cards than the Romany layout, it is considered a more complex method of cartomancy and is often preferred for querent's who have very specific questions or concerns. At the same time, it's perfectly useful for general queries or prompts that don't contain questions at all. This is a favorite spread of many professional cartomancers; it can be as simple or complex as the reader and sitter want it to be.

After shuffling and cutting your deck, you'll want to lay your cards out one at a time, face up so you can see the illustrations.

The first card you place will be the center of your cross shape--the point where the lines intersect. This is the Significator and represents the querent. It also represents current circumstances.

Second, you'll place another card on top of this, crossing it (it can be perpendicular to the first card, or laid at an angle--anything goes, so long as the first card is halfway visible beneath it). This second card represents a challenge or issue that the querent is confronting--usually the issue that is summarized by their prompt.

The third card will be laid directly beneath the first; this is the root, or foundation, of the querent's problem. It can also reference the querent's subconscious or subtextual matters that influence the issue at hand while remaining unseen, or inarticulated.

The fourth card can be placed to the left of the first; this card relates to the past, things that have expired or are currently starting to fade away.

The fifth card will be placed directly above the first; this card represents the light at the end of the tunnel, a glimmer of hope, an escape route. It is all about possibilities. It also relates to the querent's personal ambitions, plans, and aspirations.

The sixth card should be placed to the right of the first, completing the cross shape (but not the full spread). This card speaks to the near future--the next few steps, rather than the journey's final destination.

Next, you'll lay four more cards to the right of the cross in a vertical line. Start from the bottom and work your way up.

The seventh card at the bottom of this row provides advice and insight on dealing with current realities; it is the gentle push that can inspire the querent to break free of whatever has previously been holding them back and jump-start forward momentum.

The eighth card is about the querent's physical and social environment--the external factors that impact the situation, most of which are outside the querent's control.

The ninth card references both the querent's greatest hopes and deepest fears. This card points to the parts of the emotional body that most people are used to suppressing or ignoring. It may indicate that the querent has some internal work to do, or inner demons to fight before they are able to move past this problem.

The tenth card, at the top of the vertical line, will signify the ultimate outcome.

CHAPTER 12
Enhancing And Expanding

By now, we've outlined seven different options for Tarot card spreads. But there are countless others. If none of these particularly resonated with you, go ahead and keep searching. Ask fellow Tarot enthusiasts; do a web search or join an online community of cartomancers. For many generations, the methodologies of Tarot divination have been passed on through oral rather than written tradition; by talking to people who share this interest, there's no end to what you might discover.

Tarot is an art form. No matter how many spreads you have mastered or how many card meanings you have memorized, there will always be another step you could take to improve your practice and deepen your understanding.

For example, you might review the spreads in previous chapters with heightened awareness of card numbers, recognizing that a spread dominated by low card numbers may imply the situation is in its formative stages or has only just begun to unfold. By contrast, a spread dominated by high number cards indicates that the querent, or the situation they're in, is nearing the finish line; whatever's in the works will soon come to fruition, or simmering discontent will soon boil over.

You might also try reading spreads while keeping an eye out for the balance of feminine and masculine cards; as a whole, does this spread lean towards the assertive, active, and rational? Or does it lean in favor of the emotional, passive, and receptive? You could instead focus on elemental energies; upright and reversed cards; you might even read Minor Arcana cards as changing circumstances, while Major Arcana cards reference the constants or immovable realities of life.

Set goals and intentions for your readings to work towards steady improvement. Track your progress in a Tarot journal, and stay open to experimentation. Your progress may not always follow a straight, direct, forward facing line; you might have to take one step forward and then jump a few steps back to re-examine ideas that you once thought you fully understood, but now see deeper layers or hidden complexities within. There is no shame in unpacking and relearning the basics that you've already got under your belt.

Astrology and Tarot

In earlier chapters, we've already touched briefly on the correlation between Tarot and astrology. Symbols from the zodiac signs are incorporated into illustrations of several Major Arcana cards, and they are intertwined with our understanding of the four elements and the four suits that reflect them.

The world of astrology is very complex, with vast amounts of information available for interpretation. To incorporate astrology into your Tarot practice, start simple. Below is a list of the twelve signs and the cards of the Major Arcana that they are linked to, as well as their respective elements.

Aries - The Emperor - Fire

Taurus - The Hierophant - Earth

Gemini - The Lovers - Air

Cancer - The Chariot - Water

Leo - Strength - Fire

Virgo - The Hermit - Earth

Libra - Justice - Air

Scorpio - Death - Water

Sagittarius - Temperance - Fire

Capricorn - The Devil - Earth

Aquarius - The Star - Air

Pisces - The Moon - Water

The rest of the Major Arcana cards are linked to single planets or celestial bodies, rather than entire constellation signs.

Uranus - The Fool - Air

Mercury - The Magician - Air

Earth's Moon - The High Priestess - Water

Venus - The Empress - Earth

Jupiter - The Wheel of Fortune - Fire

Neptune - The Hanged Man - Water

Mars - The Tower - Fire

Earth's Sun - The Sun - Fire

Pluto - Judgement - Fire

Saturn - The World - Earth

There are further astrological correlations for all of the numbered suit and Court Cards, which can be overwhelmingly complex without a solid foundation of astrological study. Read up on the twelve zodiac signs, their seasons, and the personality traits they relate to; this information can help you make sense of confounding spreads, identify particular characters as representations of real people, and incorporate a sense of timing into your predictions.

Suits and Seasons

If you feel overwhelmed by the astrological associations of Tarot, one way to simplify the concept is to group the zodiac signs by their houses, or seasons, and correlate those to the four suits. This can allow some readers to forecast timing in a reading--for instance, alerting their sitter that the resolution of their issue may not come until the next winter season hits. Some readers are not comfortable using the cards in this way, as seasons are recurring--they may be wary of getting someone's hopes up for the coming autumn, when the cards are really pointing to an incident that will occur during the autumn season several years away, or even in the figurative autumn season of one's life (middle age). In that case, the seasonal implications of suits can simply be used to color the mood of it. Summer cards can imply easiness, carefree attitudes, and emotional warmth. Autumn cards may imply the brisk winds of change or the sense of manifestation that is embodied by the harvest season. Winter cards can point to conclusions, endings, and death, while spring cards may reference rebirth, survival, overcoming struggle, and moving on.

The suits and their respective seasons can also be connected to the four corners of the earth, though opinions on these links may vary from one cartomancer to the next. They each have correlated colors, as well.

The Suit of Wands - Spring - Fire - South - Yellow

The Suit of Cups - Summer - Water - West - Red

The Suit of Pentacles - Autumn - Earth - East - Green

The Suit of Swords - Winter - Air - North - Blue or indigo

Numerology and Tarot

Numerology is the study of symbolism and meaning in numbers. We've already touched on this in the fifth chapter, where we outlined the formula by which you can combine a suit and number to decipher a suit card's meaning.

This method can be further applied to the cards of the Major Arcana, and govern the relationships between cards within the context of a spread. For example, in a spread that features the Fool, and the Magician, as well as a Ten of Wands, the numbers one and zero in the Major Arcana could be connected to the Ten card, implying that all three cards are a part of the same narrative arc or theme. A spread that is dominated by the number ten is primarily speaking to culmination, finality, and conclusion, and since so many of these cards feature wands, you might determine that a creative endeavor is about to pay off big time.

The number zero does not factor into the interpretations of Minor Arcana cards, but it still holds a great deal of significance within numerology and the Major Arcana. It signifies freedom from responsibility, expectation, and limitation.

Addition, multiplication, and division factor heavily into this study. If you're interested in incorporating the theories of numerology into your Tarot practice, it would be wise to study numerology on its own first, and then proceed to merge the two methodologies.

Geomancy and Tarot

Geomancy is another complex and ancient divination practice. It concerns the physical alignment (or lack thereof) of items or lines in spatial relation to one another. The term "geomancy" is derived from Latin, ancient Greek, and Arabic roots, translated from words meaning "earth foresight" or "sand science."

The art of Feng Shui is an example of Geomancy; so is tasseography (the art of reading tea leaves), crystal scrying, the I Ching, Kumalak, and even rune casting. Historical evidence suggests that the earliest Geomantic methodologies arose in Africa, or possibly in ancient Arab civilizations; these methods used handfuls of dirt thrown into the air, analyzing the patterns in which they would fall, or alternatively, lines and dots drawn in the sand with the sharp end of the stick.

Geomancy incorporates the ideas of sacred geometry, numerology, mathematics, elemental physiology, geology, and astrology, using a chart of sixteen points or elemental factors. It is far too complex and extensive to outline fully within this chapter, especially as there is a great deal of recursion involved in Geomantic study (meaning that it involves terms and concepts which can only be defined by other terms and concepts that are unique to the practice--most of it is indecipherable until a student is ready to dive in and be fully immersed in the subject). I'd advise choosing one of the above-listed forms of geomancy and engaging with it as an introduction to geomantic concepts before bringing it into your Tarot practice; if you attempt to study and merge these metaphysical ideologies too quickly, you may just end up divining a headache for yourself.

Crystals, Cooking, and Creativity

If astrology, numerology, and geomancy leave you feeling boggled, numbed, or stressed, it may be time to return to the fun and carefree side of Tarot for a while.

Crystals can help to lighten the mood of your Tarot practice, as well as protect your deck from negativity. And even better--they're gorgeous! You may want to start collecting crystals with the intention of decorating a sacred space or altar in your home; they can be wonderful for meditation, yoga, reiki and chakra healing. They can also be fun to use in crafting or to wear as jewelry.

As adults, we tend to forget how we filled our days as children; without work, taxes, dating, commutes, errands, or other adult responsibilities, most of us had to get inventive and learn to entertain ourselves. We played pretend, with or without toys and costumes, and allowed our imaginations to run wild.

Both Tarot cards and crystals can be seen as toys to inspire adult play. Awaken your inner child. Throw the rules out the window. Do you feel drawn to a crystal because of its metaphysical properties, or simply because its sparkly, pretty, and you feel good when you hold it? Maybe it's the latter, but if so, who cares! Do you need a better reason?

Attraction is a fundamental form of intuition, so aim to stop questioning your impulses and desires. It's entirely possible that you like the things you like for a good reason. Whatever crystals (or bones, petrified wood, dried herbs, essential oils, or other organic materials) you find yourself drawn to are potential sources of divine inspiration. Lean into that attraction; honor it, respect it and let it guide you.

To restore some carefree fun into your Tarot practice, you might want to dabble in using the cards to source creative inspiration. Some easy examples are through cooking, painting, or creative writing. Shuffle your deck and draw cards at random to prompt your next steps--whether that dictates the ingredients you throw into a dish, the colors or shapes you choose for a blank canvas, or the characters and plot developments you use to move a fictional story forward. Some people also find Tarot cards helpful for free-writing (writing as a form of therapy, rather than writing done to create a complete narrative arc). Whatever practice you choose, you'll be amazed at how easily Tarot can reinvigorate your creative drive, helping you to think outside the box, innovate, and skip right over artistic blockages.

CONCLUSION

Thank you so much for making it through to the end of this book on Tarot. I hope it was informative, interesting, and able to provide you will all the tools you need to begin your Tarot journey. Pat yourself on the back for coming this far--it's something to be proud of, even if you still consider yourself a novice at this point.

The next step is to experiment with these techniques, and any others you might find in additional guidebooks or web sources, in order to discover what works best for you. In addition to numerology and astrology, there are many other metaphysical practices that can feed into your understanding of the Tarot deck. You might want to look into crystal healing, and discover which crystals can help to absorb or deflect negativity, protecting your deck and your readings from dark energies. Alternatively, you might work with geomancy grids; you might incorporate Tarot into your meditation practice, reiki sessions, or chakra healing; you could use your cards in Pagan or Wiccan ceremonial rites.

Beyond the metaphysical realm, Tarot can still be useful; some creative writers draw cards at random as writing prompts, or in order to plot out the next leg of their protagonist's journey. Those who are spiritually or esoterically minded might adopt the practice of shuffling and drawing a card at random every morning, using the Tarot to guide them through each day of their life's journey.

The possibilities for expanding and enhancing your intuition are truly endless.

Finally, if you enjoyed this book, please take a moment to rate it on Amazon. Your honest review would be greatly appreciated. Thank you!

DESCRIPTION

Tarot cards have been in use for over five hundred years, for gameplay, divination, creative inspiration and spiritual practice. The practice of reading Tarot comes with a rich, complex history, full of mystical, philosophical, and religious mystery. As old as the art form may be, its popularity in modern culture is growing rapidly; Tarot decks and cartomancy play a significant role in many present-day metaphysical healing practices, spiritual training, as well as artistic and creative circles.

With detailed illustrations and cryptic symbolism, Tarot can easily pique your interest--but where should you begin? There is an overwhelming amount of information out there, and since Tarot is an esoteric practice, it's difficult to know which sources have enough authority to provide accurate and reliable instruction.

In truth, there is no right way to use Tarot, nor is there a wrong way. The practice of cartomancy is all about intuition. If you don't consider yourself a deeply intuitive person, then the cards can be used to enhance your emotional instincts. Alternatively, if you are already guided by your visceral sensations, you might use Tarot to articulate and explain your gut instincts, elevating the things you feel to things you believe, understand, or "know."

The only way to know how useful and impactful Tarot could be in your life is to try it. Roll up your sleeves and dive in, whether you already have a deck or are simply considering how and where to acquire one. The best time to get started is right now.

In this book you will learn:

- What Tarot is, and how you can use it

- The history, legends, myths, and lore of Tarot's origins

- How to choose and acquire your first deck (hint: don't purchase it for yourself!)

- How and where to store your Tarot deck

- How to cleanse your cards
- How to awaken, nurture, and strengthen your intuitive gifts
- How to interpret all the cards of the Major Arcana
- How to read all of the cards within the Minor Arcana
- How to decipher the meanings of reversed cards
- How to determine the meanings of suits and their respective elements
- How to interpret cards in groups, allowing them to impact each other
- How to read simple one, two and three card spreads
- How to layout complex and traditional spreads, such as the Romany and Celtic Cross spreads
- How to incorporate astrology, numerology, geomancy, and other metaphysical practices into your Tarot work
- And more...

www.ingramcontent.com/pod-product-compliance
Lightning Source LLC
Chambersburg PA
CBHW071458070526
44578CB00001B/379